First edition 2014
Author: Wilfried Ehrmann
Cover design, illustration: © Creativeapril – fotolia.com
Translation: Michael Ehrmann
Publisher: tao.de in J. Kamphausen Mediengruppe GmbH, Bielefeld,
www.tao.de, eMail: info@tao.de
ISBN:
978-3-95802-174-7 (Paperback)
978-3-95802-175-4 (Hardcover)
978-3-95802-176-1 (e-Book)
First published in German 2011 by J. Kamphausen-Verlag, Bielefeld,
titled: "Vom Mut zu wachsen. Sieben Stufen der integralen Heilung"

Wilfried Ehrmann

Consciousness in Evolution

Seven Steps of Integral Healing

Translation: Michael Ehrmann

Table of Contents

Foreword by the Editor

Who am I? Who could I be? It is questions like these that remind us of the essential quality of personhood, of the fact that in life we are on an inner path of growth - whether as an individual growing from a baby into an adult, or as an entire species evolving from the ape into present-day homo sapiens – the sensible, wise man. Through a unique interplay between the inner drive and external demands we have become what we are today: being aware that we have not yet reached the end of our path.

With this book, Wilfried Ehrmann has drawn a detailed map of the connections between consciousness, culture and evolution, which shows where we come from and where to we can grow. Being a psychotherapist, he is well acquainted with the inner dynamics of the psyche and connects these internal worlds with external existence. He demonstrates how in the intertwined personal and cultural perspectives, through our own interaction with the systems we have established, the Here and Now may take shape, the legacy of the past may live on, and the potential of the future may appear as a beacon on the horizon.

In this multitude of perspectives, which in integral theory is represented by the four quadrants, the author focusses on the developments that happen at the interfaces between the respective spheres. How does the culture we live in affect the way in which we perceive the world? How do the institutions we have established influence our minds? What opportunities for development are there, and where do we come up against limiting factors?

These reflections show that a frequent motivation for further growth is fear. When at our present stage of development we fail to see a possibility of fulfilling our needs, we start to explore virgin territories, hoping to find safety and fulfilment in those new places.

To Wilfried Ehrmann, this upward movement involves seven stages in the development of consciousness, which apply both to the historical development of mankind and the essentials of individual development.

In coordinated practical exercises he shows how our environment may help us grow and how our inner transformation not only benefits us but moreover represents a helpful impetus for other people.

Just as our individual abilities grow more and more varied from day one to adulthood, so does the variety of values and systems increase on a cultural or social dimension.

While integral theory clearly distinguishes between different aspects of development, defining independent patterns of development for each of these elements, the author's aim is to point out general dynamics of evolution and to show the interplay between the different areas.

This meta-perspective makes the discrimination of integral theory (whose aim it is to achieve greater discriminatory power between categories and to avoid reductionisms) fade into the background for the sake of an overall picture and a focus on interconnectedness.

The author takes us on an exciting journey, which leads us from the roots of human existence to the glowing vista of future unity. He points out a path of liberation and healing, which leads us to our true self and opens up new possibilities for the development of humanity as a species.

Dr. Nadja Rosmann

Editor of „Integrale Reihe"

Foreword by the Author

The entire history of mankind affects our inner life, mostly without our knowledge. Often this influence on our soul is so subtly and finely ingrained in our patterns of behaviour that we view them as a matter of course, unaware that and how they separate us from what we really want and what is important to us.

In a way, our personal life story represents a miniature repetition of human cultural development in general. The challenges we are confronted with our individual lives are similar to those that all mankind has had to take up. Thus, we can learn from our precursors in history how we might succeed in life but also how we might fail.

However, we "repeat" history in our own individual way. It is not a blind repetition of a process that has happened a million times before, but rather a rewriting of history in our own personal style. Yet, it also involves the continuation of historical developments in new areas made accessible by a new personal history. Being aware of this makes us feel unique as well as connected with a long and great history, both at the same time.

The model of the evolution of consciousness allows us to put into broader contexts unresolved issues from our past that burden us, allotting to them a point of reference from history. Then we will know where to begin with the confrontation, which could be accompanied with the specific exercises in this book.

Thus, our study of the evolution of consciousness need not be a mere acquisition of knowledge. We can use it to work towards personal transformation. We can apply it in the hope that it may enable us to see more clearly the roots of our reactions, problems and motives, and gain a deeper understanding of ourselves and the people around us.

If we want to make progress on our path to realisation and liberation, we first have to know what the major tasks of each stage of consciousness are. What we fail to achieve at one stage we will miss at the next. Once we understand the model we will know where to go back to if we have got stuck somewhere. Once we are there we will know what to make up for so we may acquire a new resource.

Finally, the model of the evolution of consciousness shows that while there is some point in achieving most of the things we want to achieve in life, we will not always be striving for the highest. The deepest inner quest is the quest for oneness. Its goal is something eternal, something leading not to short-term satisfaction but to genuine serenity: something that brings inner peace and exorcises fear.

The power that inspires in us the desire for progress and freedom from pressure and contraction knows what it is to be in harmony with the world and supported by love. We carry this knowledge deep within our hearts. It belongs to us as individuals, and it belongs to the legacy of mankind, being the essence of ancient texts, repeated and re-edited again and again through the ages, in all cultures.

If we resolve to move on towards this great goal, the model of the evolution of consciousness is to encourage us to stick to this path and keep on walking, like the entire human species. Each depiction of a stage of evolution is therefore followed with a small section devoted to reflection and exercises. This will give us the opportunity to gain a deeper awareness of our own personal evolutionary history.

This book will take you on a journey of discovery. On this trip, some things already familiar to you may appear in a new guise. You will explore virgin territory, reaching vantage points exposing to view vast, uncharted territories of your life.

Sometimes, your path may lead through dry and barren landscapes, whose beauty you will acknowledge only if you stay a while. You will come to exciting and unexpected places, especially if you do the exercises of introspection at the end of each chapter. This journey is meant to give you heart: heart to confront what so far you may have been trying to evade; heart to move on with a commitment to improve on your own life. Reading this book may lend you a deeper understanding of how invaluable the legacy of history within your soul is – it is a rich heritage that can be used for stimulation in everyday life, in relationships and for whatever you do. You will realise that this legacy provides you with the resources that are required in the future. Just as human cultural consciousness steadily grows and develops further, so does the evolution of your personal life follow an inner plan, whose stages this book may help you see more clearly. This book is meant to encourage you to put your trust in the power of the evolution of consciousness, so that with care and confidence you may master the varied tasks you are presented with in this world.

Culture, Consciousness, and Evolution – an Introduction

Models of the development of consciousness have something fascinating about themselves as they allow to combine a vision of history with our personal lives. In this task, two fields of tension have to be mastered: Models should be generalizing to a degree that facts and phenomena can find their place easily. They should reach as far into details as is needed to get a precise sense of the peculiarities of a certain level.

Furthermore, the steps from level to level should mark the progression of development in which the present circumstances are overcome by something completely new. At the same time, the continuous development of the whole should be conceivable at any point. So the model should contain steps which should follow one after the other in a plausible way while marking a difference among themselves and obey a general pattern of movement as well.

The model of spiral dynamics has enchanted me due to its inner logics and its combination of simplicity and complexity. It originates from the findings of the US psychologist Clare Graves (1914 – 1986). He writes: "The psychology of the mature human being is an unfolding, emergent, oscillating, spiraling process marked by progressive subordination of older, lower-order behaviour systems to newer, higher-order systems as man's existential problems change."

Grave's model is an enhancement of the well-known motivation pyramid by Abraham Maslow and wants to serve as a summing-up of different models of evolution. It bears certain similarities to other step ladders like those from Jean Gebser and Ken Wilber. Going further back, we can probably find G.F.W. Hegel's "Phenomenology of Spirit" as prototype.

After thorough study of the system, I have applied some changes which deemed important to me. They can add to a better comprehensibility and applicability of the model.

Cultural Evolution and Consciousness

The history of the evolution of nature does not end with its culmination in the appearance of the homo sapiens. Though admittedly for 40.000 years there have been no significant changes in its genetic substratum, the appearance of the homo sapiens is just the beginning of an equally exciting development, in whose course he will overthrow the Earth, create great art, come up with ever new technological refinements, kill millions of his own kind and try out myriads of ideas on how to lead a better life. The subject of this book is the homo sapiens on the path to himself. Just as in his preceding natural history man had to go through diverse stages in order to arrive at his present level of biological evolution, he must also pass through various stages in the course of his cultural development if he is to fulfil what in his heart he knows to be his destiny.

The definition of the term evolution, which Charles Darwin first introduced to natural science, is simplified here. In the context of this book, evolution is defined in the following way: it denotes that there are different cultural stages that build on one another (with later ones always requiring and necessitating earlier ones), and that these stages have to be passed through in succession.

Avoiding the notion of coincidence, which is central to Darwin's concept of natural selection, we will instead be discussing evolution in terms of the opposite notion of necessity. However, it is not always possible or necessary to know beforehand what the steps of evolution are going to be. Cultural evolution does not follow along the lines of any kind of predictable logic. The necessity in question is not that of a law of classical natural science.

Therefore, tribal structures can continue to exist today in some regions of the world, while in other places they disintegrated 12.000 years ago. Yet, it is now almost beyond doubt that even the few remaining communities that still retain their Stone Age way of life sooner or later will have to develop on to the next stages of evolution, whether they or we like it or not.

It is, however, not a case of rigid necessity. In the course of cultural evolution there have been so many retrograde steps, sideward movements, and dead ends that the concept of systematic progress, following a pattern of thesis, antithesis and synthesis, seldom applies. The necessity we claim here is based on observations of human history and ourselves, of our deepest wishes and desires. It is revealed in our strife for what alleviates suffering in us as individuals or in larger or smaller groups.

Cultural development involves two dimensions: that of individual purpose (that which individuals aspire to or avoid) and that of the social structure (textures composed of what different individuals aspire to and avoid).

What a person wants or doesn't want is influenced by what people around him want or don't want. Also, his aspirations depend on what is called for by the natural environment. Finally, they should also be seen in connection with the requirements of the self-regulatory system of our inner world. All these mutual influences give rise to what has been termed "culture". It is the basic models of these interactions that are discussed here.

What is meant by consciousness in the context of this book is one's inner culture. We always experience culture directly, and consequently our consciousness – i.e. the form and content of our experience – is suffused with it. Most cultural stages discussed in this book are also highly influential elements of individual experience. Our experience of culture becomes imminent in the way in which we perceive ourselves. Thus, the views of an Inuit woman of herself and the world will be different from those of a woman from Afghanistan or one from India.

Every stage of consciousness encompasses all experienced reality. Therefore, it can be portrayed only in an exemplary manner, and aided by these examples the reader may associatively deepen her understanding of herself. There can be no complete reconstruction of any of the stages but there are basic ideas we may point to.

How people move, how they use language, what they do and what they don't do, what they think and what they don't think – all this is influenced by the respective stage of consciousness. Frequently, of course, all we can do is conjecture; the aim, however, is really to develop a consistent idea that may be elaborated, completed, or reinforced.

We shall also be reconstructing motives and driving forces behind actions: we shall be describing key emotions and important patterns of motivations. Every individual action reflects the consciousness that caused it, and every motive has the characteristics of the cultural structure it is embedded in.

The notion of stages of consciousness is meant metaphorically and refers to a sequence along the lines of a certain logic of development. What is not meant is that as soon as a new level has been reached everything changes and what went before is forgotten. Instead, old structures will continue to exist parallel to the achievements of the new stage, and their status will change in the face of the new organisation of human experience. Thus, in this model of history there do exist overlaps and concurrences. It is also a model of progress from a "lower" to a "higher" state, involving an increase in complexity where the "lower" is embedded in the "higher". The premise is thus that complexity increases the further you go along the time line.

The notion of stages should be taken metaphorically also in the sense that man's inner development is somewhat analogous to it. Frequently, we comprehend important stages in our personal development in terms of old patterns losing their power and a new stage being reached that is superior to the old one and that we therefore hold on to, until it is possible to move on to yet a higher stage. If a child is proficient at the essential aspects of his mother tongue, then the previous system of communication via pre-lingual means has lost its central status although it will never completely disappear; and, given a healthy development, there will be no backslide from the level of differentiated communication.

In groups and larger systems of community (including whole cultures), such major steps in the development happen much more slowly and cover longer periods of time. Thus, in a continual historical record they will scarcely be noticeable, as with parents, who will not notice bigger steps in the growth of their children as clearly as those who see them only every now and then will. Cultures, too, undergo such changes as they develop. In this book, their relevance and interaction with the developments on an individual level are discussed.

Our deepest feelings and strongest impulses stem from the eldest stratums of human experience. Therefore, an understanding of the dynamics of the stages of consciousness may help us explain our own attitudes, feelings, and actions. All the stages reverberate within every one of us as memories of the collective soul. If we learn how to differentiate between them – how to realise which of our inner voices is speaking to us from what level of consciousness - it will be easier for us to keep things in order within. We will discover that sometimes we attempt to solve a problem belonging to a more complex stage of consciousness with the tools of an earlier stage, and we will no longer have to wonder why we are not succeeding.

For instance, imagine a conflict in a relationship where the one person is called upon to understand the needs and wishes of the other, which are topics of stage five. If we use the energy of stage two, an aggressive escalation of the conflict is likely to ensue. If we use the power of stage three, the question of who is right and who is wrong will be in the foreground of the argument. If we, however, search for the resources of more complex stages, such as those of systemic consciousness, we will find it easier to acquire a deeper understanding of what the other person's needs and wishes are.

The power at work behind the scenes of evolution can be explained with a water analogy. Imagine a new spring flowing out of a mountain. Although the water urges onward, its course is not linear: like a spiral, it moves backwards and forwards. The path of the water is unpredictable in its detail: there are bound to be many surprises. Therefore, we cannot know the exact course of the water beforehand and are equally ignorant of how long it will take: what we do know is that there is a goal which the water from the spring will eventually reach, becoming one with the ocean.

The Stages of Evolution from a Cultural Viewpoint

The biological prequel of the history of mankind, from the beginnings of life in single-celled organisms to the more complex life-forms offers certain basics that help explain the dynamic forces behind the cultural development of man. The self-organisation of life, with its polarity of growth and insurance of survival, is embedded in a web of cooperation and communication. Thus, the axes of human history are inherent already in the earliest forms of life. The years given below refer to the early beginnings of the respective stage. The process of the complete realisation of a stage takes very long, sometimes hundreds or thousands of years.

Stage 1 (tribal):

Man is a community-building creature (*zoon politicon* in the words of Aristotle). He could not survive without living with his fellow species. The closest cousins to the homo sapiens, the primates, too, are highly social. To retain a certain group structure, man introduces social rules and rituals. Tradition has a significant role, and information is transmitted primarily via narratives. The individual has to subordinate herself to group interests. The elders are given "higher" status than younger people. The group's habitat is limited to essentials, and it is very closely connected to nature.

Stage 2 (emancipatory/individualistic) – from ca. 10.000 BC:

The rise of agriculture causes a break with tribal lifestyle and tradition. Thus, some individuals, who in mythology are referred to as heroes, leave the closed system of the traditional tribe. Questioning the old traditions, they desire to introduce new values. They strive for independence and personal freedom. They build up strong emotions providing motivation for their actions. In the historical record, they appear as the first surviving names. In ancient Greece, this form of consciousness almost explosively gains widespread acceptance.

Stage 3 (bureaucratic/hierarchical) – from ca. 3.000 BC:

In his urge for expansion, the hero comes up against limiting factors and is forced to make way for a new system of organisation. States and empires are created, which rule over a great number of people with the help of their hierarchical structures. Free emotional expression is curtailed by new laws. Violence is monopolised. The state is invented and perfected. A handful of religions (including the world religions of today) spread far and wide. The beginnings of this stage can be found in the advanced cultures of antiquity.

Stage 4 (materialistic) – from ca. 1.500 AD

This stage involves the development of the principles of rationality and effectivity. Cost-benefit calculations are dominant in thinking. The strife for individual advantage and profit becomes a central maxim. Every man is the architect of his own fortune (in every possible sense of the word), and the state is disempowered to a great extent. The liberal game of power not only dominates the market but has a great influence on the organisation of community. Everything in view is thought of as potential object of exploitation. In Europe, the beginnings of this stage go back to the blossoming of urban culture in the late middle ages.

Stage 5 (personalistic) – from ca. 1750 AD:

Being a person involves much more than mere economic development. The dictate of profit maximisation is opposed by the creative development of the multidimensional person. Capitalism is criticised for being a system of alienation. Life is regarded as a once-only chance of personal fulfilment. Every person is regarded as unmistakable and unique – and, as such, invaluable. These ideas are formulated primarily by the early proponents of Enlightenment.

Stage 6 (systemic) – from ca. 1950 AD:

The systemic point of view transcends the individual person. The basic realisation is that the only way in which we may develop yet further and solve all our problems is if we gain insight into the complex web of interrelated motivations and interests. The insight into the interdependence of all actions gains a paradigmatic value. All stages previous are integrated with all their respective particularities and needs, and none of them will exert power over the others. Global conferences and world organisations indicate this stage.

Stage 7 (holistic):

The systemic viewpoint can be implemented in society only if it is represented and practised by people with personal integrity. Personal integrity is based on the insight that all other stages of consciousness are limited, and on the realisation that they can be transcended via personal transformation, inter alia by overcoming the fears and desires that perpetuate the other stages. Then, the focus of life changes, and actions are determined by what is called for at the present moment. All other stages of consciousness have their place, without any one of them putting itself in the foreground or wielding authority over the others. In our day, more and more spiritual teachers make their appearance, raising the spirit of a tolerant and profound humanity and motivating people to make peace with themselves and their environment.

The Stages of Individual Development

How do the stages of evolution manifest in our personal history?

Stage 1 (tribal) – first year of life

The infant is born into a community (family), where from the very beginning it develops feelings of belonging. Feelings of security and trust increase likewise.

Stage 2 (emancipatory/individualistic) – second year of life

From its first year of life, the self-awareness of the child evolves, and it starts to demand from the parents and contradict the family's rules and expectations.

Stage 3 (bureaucratic/hierarchical) – fourth year of life

At the age of four to five years, the infant develops an understanding for rules and authorities. Role play serves to simulate dominance and submission. In modern society, these experiences help to prepare for schooling.

Stage 4 (materialistic) – early school age

At around the sixth year of life, the infant begins to develop a realistic world view that greatly differs from the magical world of the little child. Its contact with the material world comes to the fore. The child begins to learn and understand the workings of a world so demanding of the individual. Performance motivation originates, and so does the formula of competition. These values, too, are in part formed by school education.

Stage 5 (personalistic) – puberty

In puberty, the child becomes an adult and maturely self-aware. The individual person takes shape and reflects on her own growth, independently of the expectations and ideas of her parents, her peers, or the society and culture at large.

Stage 6 (systemic) – adulthood

With the coming of age, the awareness of global issues rises and the ability to think systemically increases. Issues are now viewed from various angles, and things are judged in an increasingly differentiated manner. Life is seen as part of a broader picture, and commitment to making the world a better place begins.

Stage 7 (holistic):

Interest in spirituality links back to the earlier magical thinking and to periods of doubt and search for meaning. Crises frequently help strengthen the faith in a higher power and wisdom. There may be single experiences of holistic consciousness already in early childhood. Later in life, what it usually requires is a devotedness to working on one's fears and opening up to a deeper level of human experience.

Stage seven does not belong to any one age in particular: there are those who begin their spiritual journey at a very young age, those who embark on it later in life, and those who never really set out for it. In traditional Hinduist culture, however, there is a time reserved for it: at the age of 65 or 70, the old family man, businessman or politician may give up his worldly life, take up a begging bowl and retire to a cave for meditation.

The Organic Foundations of Life and Evolution

Human life is based on biological processes resulting from billions of years of evolution. The genesis of human life represents a qualitative leap bringing the phenomenon of culture to this planet. Culture is here defined as a form of social interaction of self-aware living beings that results in an organisation of community and the exertion of influence on the natural environment. In prehuman forms of life we can make out the structures of consciousness (which is a crucial factor for man's cultural achievements) in their simplest possible form. Therefore, it may be helpful at this point to briefly discuss the organic preconditions of cultural development.

Organic consciousness denotes the ruling principle of fundamental vital processes. The original form of life is represented by individual cells. Every cell is capable of learning. This quality is an important parameter for the success of the cell in widening its area of life. We may assume that the beginnings of communication occurred at the stage of individual cells. The cell's organelles exchange information and organise their activities in reaction to the input they receive. Thus, there will be an exchange of data, questions and answers, orders and confirmations, maybe even encouragement, praise or criticism. Verbal communication as practised by man is thus a further development of these basic forms from the organic level. Here we have the basis for all the succeeding stages of evolution. What this suggests is that an inner logical consistency is inherent in evolution. It unfolds what is already built into the simplest forms of life into ever greater complexity.

The Biological Foundation of Religion

Here is an example: the foundation of religion is the self-regulation of the vital processes in every form of organic life. Every single part fulfils its obligations according to a master plan, which none of the individual parts can influence and which ensures the sustenance of the system. Each element plays its part with the "consciousness" that is granted it in the overall systematic context and that it can never fully understand – which is not necessary for the fulfilment of a subtask. However, what is necessary is a linkage (*religio*) with the whole, an awareness that every individual part must fulfil its obligation trusting that the system on the whole will know what it takes to ensure survival.

Each individual element knows that there is a master plan, lacking however the capability of comprehending this plan and knowing all its details. But it is also aware that it could not survive if there were no master plan. This, then, is how important it is to be linked to the whole.

We may conclude that the existence of what will later be referred to as the divine is structurally inherent in every living being. All religious creeds are derived from these basic structures. The religious expression of these fundamental structures depend on the demands of life and the historical context, according to what benefits the whole and enables the individual to contribute to it.

The basic idea, then, is that there is something higher that creates life (the divine Creator) and sustains it in spite of its complexity (God the Sustainer). Human being lacks the cognitive capacity and the intelligence necessary for decoding the master plan. Nevertheless, they have got what it takes to understand that there must be a plan and that a higher power, which is "beyond" the capacities of the human mind, is responsible for it.

Man's insight, then, is that there are certain limits to human perception, and therefore all he can do is trust that the Divine Being beyond these limits acts in a "good", responsible way. If man is to serve the whole (and consequently himself), his actions must depend on where his limits are. Human action is destructive or evil where there is the misconception that the purpose is common good while selfish interests are hidden under this guise of innocence – like cells that merely follow their own plan without corresponding to the whole, thus endangering the health of the system with their uncontrolled growth.

From this point of view, man is just as religious as any other living being is. This makes the explicit practice of religion plausible. However, one result of the evolution of the mind is the ability to doubt anything, even one's vital basis, which may give rise to various kinds of atheistic or agnostic "belief systems".

Growth State and Protective State

Life forms, from single-celled organisms to the most complex mammals, have a certain basic structure that adjusts their inner balance to the conditions of the environment. If a system is located in a conducive environment – if, say, a single-celled organism swims in a nutrient solution –, then all the processes of metabolism will take place in an ideal manner, and the living being can freely develop according to its own inner build.

This state may therefore be referred to as growth state. Transient and little challenges that cause stress belong to this category as well, because they have a conducive effect on one's commitment and motivation.

If the environmental conditions change, the organism must protect itself in order to secure its survival. It will muster all its strength to confront the danger or escape it (fight or flight). Stress mechanisms will be activated. This is referred to as a protective state.

In the fortunate case, the organism manages to eliminate or escape the danger and may return to its normal level of energy and to a growth state. In the unfortunate case, the organism will be subject to grievous, persisting strain, use up important resources and may degenerate or even die. The third possibility is that the state of endangerment cannot be ended but is not strong enough to destroy the organism. In this case, the protective state will gain predominance and the possibilities of the growth state are restricted. Over time, the organism will be subject to insidious drain, as more resources are used up than ~~are~~ built up. The protective state must be abandoned sometime, or the organism will die of exhaustion.

The Foundation of Human Emotions

These are the two fundamental states of all living organisms at any stage of evolution. From a certain stage onwards they are felt as emotions. The growth state corresponds to all emotions we like refer to as "positive". These are the emotions that inspire growth – love-related growth (when we are falling in love or taking care of children), worldly growth (when we are successful and projects have been completed), creative growth (when we are having ideas or have created something new), or growth of consciousness (when we experience peak states or religious revelations). The biological preconditions for this state and for the emotions corresponding to it are provided by a part of the nervous system that only mammals possess, which is responsible for the coordination of social activities ("smart vagus").

The protective state corresponds to all emotions that we like to refer to as bad or negative. Chief amongst these emotions is fear, which causes feelings of limitation and tension. Fear is the opposite pole to the expansion and freedom we experience in a state of love and creativity. Derivatives from fear are feelings like anger (for defence in cases of emergency), sadness (for processing a loss or a danger overcome), or disgust (for protection against harmful influences). The occurrence of such feelings, which we may refer to as protective feelings, indicates that we are under threat and driven by fear. They are a root of dysfunctional perception (our perception is restricted in such a state) and action (our behavioural repertoire is significantly reduced, including in essence all possible variants of fight or flight). The sympathetic nervous system is responsible for this state, whose fight-flight pattern can already be found in simple living organisms.

Of course, emotions develop on from these roots. The human need to communicate requires a broad spectrum of emotions, which are used as signals for communication. In challenging situations, however, we tend to fall back on deeply ingrained, simple emotions.

Two Driving Forces of Evolution

This duality of inner states hints at the two driving forces of evolution, which motivate the evolution of consciousness. On the one hand, there are the forces of growth, which on expansion must come up against a limiting factor on the level of the individual cell. The clustering of several cells into groups and thus the development towards a new, a higher level of organisation is fuelled by this dynamic force. On the other hand, there are the powers of protection. They work to overcome the dangerous scenarios that appear insurmountable at the present level by trying out a new form of organisation.

The second form can only be successful if at the newly acquired stage of organisation enough creative resources can be provided after its establishment for extending and stabilising, as it were, the bridgehead in the new territory. Otherwise, this evolutionary step will be unsuccessful and things will return to the way they were before.

The incredible diversity of nature, the large and small wonders that it can offer to the observer, express their immeasurably creative powers. Every blossom in its exuberant beauty shows how the plant is celebrating its own growth and fertility. When we experience beauty, we express our amazement about the abundance and wealth that flow from an inexhaustible source of creativity.

Fear cannot correctly be referred to as the driving factor of evolution. Admittedly, at all stages of consciousness but the last one, fears play a dominant and formative part. They narrow perception and mind. Every stage endeavours to overcome the fears specific to the one that went before and to come to terms with the fears felt at the new stage. The status quo of relative ease with these fears, however, cannot last forever, as with a dam which continuously exposed to flood waters will finally give in.

Then there will be times of crisis and upheaval. What is new must take up the challenge of breaking through, like the baby who, in spite of considerable risks and hardship, must make its way through the birth canal. Massive fears are felt during such periods of transition, but there are also strong impulses of moving forwards, which prove superior to the fears once the breakthrough has been successfully achieved.

Eventually, then, it is the impulse of growth which is active behind the coping attempts of fear. Thus, human creativity as a whole could be understood as a great undertaking to ban the fears. Creative efforts are rewarded with feelings of happiness as inherent in any achievement realised in spite of fear-laden inhibitions. With every moment of liberation, new creative power is unleashed, which in turn can be used in the course of further evolutionary progress.

For a new stage of consciousness to be reached, then, two aspects are indispensable: the creativity we owe to the growth state and the protection provided by the survival-ensuring protective state. Without the phases of growth life would stagnate and shrivel at any given level. A growth state is a state of experimentation and variation, like a painter who trying out different shades of a colour eventually finds the mixture ideal for his purposes. Steps into new stages are taken on a trial basis, as with an explorer who hits upon uncharted territory and enters it for the first time. Caution is here required, as the potential dangers at the new stage are as yet unknown. The explorer must reckon with the existence of fell beasts on the newly discovered island, and must therefore be on the alert. Should he go about it too carelessly, he will quickly fail on his mission of the creative new beginning. But without the factor of overflowing courage, as connected with this creative step, he will not even think of looking for unknown islands.

As we have said, every stage of consciousness is confronted with a specific form of fear. This fear causes the characteristic limitations of the perception of the time, influencing emotional patterns and thought structures as well as the choice of available alternatives for action. From this repertoire, with its respective limitations, the basic matrix of individual forms of society and cultural spheres is constructed. Every culture, then, has a reality of its own, which is created by specifically narrowed, fear-determined ways of perceiving the world.

The "real" reality reveals itself only to the unreserved, fear-free point of view, which is possible at the seventh stage of consciousness. According to Indian philosophy, this perspective is the product of the liberation from *maya*, the veil of illusion.

The Seven Stages of Consciousness

Stage 1: Tribal Consciousness – Humanity as Belonging Together

Every part of this earth is sacred to my people. Every shining pine needle, every sandy shore, every mist in the dark woods, every clearing and humming insect is holy in the memory and experience of my people. The sap, which courses through the trees, carries the memories of the red man.

Chief Seattle

Key aspects:
community and belonging, tradition and ritual, love of nature, fear for survival

> *Tokolu is sitting in the circle of his tribe around a fire. There is laughter and light conversation. The children are running around, playing amongst the adults. The smaller ones are seated near Kanabai, enraptured by her tales – tales about the raven man, about forest spirits and rain-makers.*
>
> *In a few days, the ritual will commence that is to initiate him into adult life. If he succeeds, he will be sitting with the men and joining their hunt. He has learnt to handle bow and arrow and to throw his spear with deadly accuracy.*
>
> *The ritual will be tough and challenging, but he is looking forward to it. If he succeeds, the girls will admire him for it. He takes a look around. Everyone who is sitting here around the fire is known to him: all those familiar faces, laughs, and quips. He is one of them. He feels safe within the circle of his tribe.*

Ritualized Communities

The leap from solitude to company – where one is connected with the other – is taken where individual cells unite to form groups. The step is taken because cells are incapable of expanding beyond a certain size. To ensure their own survival, they must overcome their "individualistic" self and form coalitions with other cells. Multicellular organisms evolve, which function on the basis of division of labour.

As intracellular processes follow certain communicative rules, the interactions taking place within the individual cells must be translated to other cells. Various languages are therefore developed, from electro-chemical languages of signals to man's highly complex languages of symbols.

With the emergence of human life, communication becomes indispensable, and language must be transformed into something more than mere idioglossia. What goes hand in glove with these developments is the creation of binding rules that regulate interaction. On the organic level already, it is inacceptable in a cell that is responsible for, say, reproduction to work instead for excretion, or vice versa. The cells will remain a group only if each fulfils its special designated obligations.

The tribal idea that social rules have priority over individual impulses derives from the wisdom of organic consciousness. However, it is still a new beginning: for the first time self-aware, reflective living beings walk the Earth, whose cultural achievements set them apart from all other creatures.

Culture is here defined simply as the organisation of the social life of reflective creatures. Reflective creatures are beings capable of experiencing themselves (internal communication), other members of their species (social communication), and both at the same time (cultural communication). Culture begins where the history of mankind begins.

When animals and people cluster in groups, the necessary social rules and implications are already known to them due to earlier phases of evolution. Therefore, they do not need to learn from scratch what a rule is and why rules should be followed. In fact, every child has an intuitive knowledge about rules, which it draws from its communicative experiences with the environment, which follow predictable patterns. Even though a child does not always want to understand or follow the rules, they still provide it with a sense of safety and support.

This example also shows that the meaning of a rule – and by extension the meaning of a culture – is not set to begin with but must be learned. In contrast to the multicellular organism, a community does not have a centre of coordination that can simply "make" all individual elements work together in the same way as a bird can cause all the necessary cells to cooperate when it wants to spread its wings. Within a community, harmony must be established by its members, and this is also why people develop languages, using them on a regular basis to sustain and improve the quality of social life. This is why people frequently discuss the same subject over and over without actually exchanging additional information. Such redundancies serve to ensure and heighten the sense of community within a group.

The Concept of the Social Contract

We may be inclined to think of a tribe as a crowd of individual people who have allied themselves for a certain purpose. However, this does not quite reflect the spirit of tribal communities but is a retrospective projection of the insolating mindset of materialistic consciousness (stage 4). The concept of the social contract of Thomas Hobbes and Jean Jacques Rousseau is based on the materialistic view of man, suggesting that at the beginning of human history individuals voluntarily joined to form a community, yielding their individual power to a central leadership.

For man in his early days, however, the idea of solitariness was connected with the notion of inevitable death. In fact, human life was seen as an expression of community. It was felt that life is only possible within a tribal community. Man's identification with the tribe was connected with his understanding of his own viability and right to live. From a tribal point of view, the idea of a solitary individual is "abstract", i.e. not supported by what is actually experienced.

Tribal consciousness acknowledges the distinguishing personal traits of individual members, which are frequently reflected in their names. Everyone is free to be the way he wants to be but must follow the rules of the tribe, which cannot be changed. For these rules provide the framework for all productive and reproductive processes; and people are afraid that questioning these basic conditions of tribal community life may endanger the tribe itself and all its members.

What the individual members of the tribe have in common is given priority over what distinguishes them: individual differences are seen only as varieties of common ground. Within this framework, there is no great motivation for the cultivation of specialized or unusual talents or skills. This is why tribal forms of community may survive for thousands (if not millions) of years without major alterations of their rules and traditions.

The sense of unity felt within a tribe is heightened by its emotional enclosure from the outside world. People from other tribes are viewed as strangers and are mistrusted. They speak differently, they have other tales and rituals and treat nature differently. Their alterity is regarded as a threat to the tribe's traditional way of life and is therefore devalued. The notion of personhood is reserved exclusively for one's own group, which reflects in the fact that many of the names for individual tribes correspond to the term for mankind in the respective languages. If members of other tribes are integrated – as through marriage – they are "re-educated", i.e. instructed in the characteristic traditions of the tribe.

The Nature-Man Continuum

Fully fledged tribal consciousness took effect in the social structure of the tribes of the Stone Age, which for millions of years ensured the passing on of the human genome and gradually explored new habitats all over the globe.

One quality of these communities is their close relationship to the natural environment, which is reflected in their considerable knowledge of it. This knowledge is "narrative", i.e. embedded in a narrative structure with causal explanations. It can be acquired and applied solely in the context of the narrative form of the respective tribe. Other tribes apply very different kinds of tales to explain the enigmas of the world and the problems encountered in daily life.

The relationship of early cultures to nature is characterised not by contrast but, to put it in modern terms, by a kind of partnership. For instance, the concept of sacrifice, as prevalent among these tribal communities, is based on the assumption that nature must be compensated for what is taken from it. Thus, tribal communities barter, as it were, with nature in the spirit of fairness.

These people communicated with nature in ways now widely unknown to us. If we can actually communicate verbally with birds and beasts, then the boundary between man and nature must be much more open than we now imagine it to be. The weaker the boundary is defined as, the easier it is to harmonize with the other side.

For Stone Age man, his close contact with the environment was central. If the signs of nature could be read and their messages decoded successfully, it was also possible to get answers to one's questions from nature. Then, undesirable changes in nature could be dealt with successfully.

Tradition

Tradition is one of the key aspects of tribal consciousness, transferring the conservatism of nature to the tribal sphere. Tradition includes all knowledge that the tribe needs to ensure its own survival. Information is passed down orally and in an illustrative way. Therefore, there will be no doubt in its correctness. The elders are highly respected within the tribe and make the important decisions. Since the survival skills handed down are central to tribal life, the ancestors, too, are respected and honoured. Various tales keep their memory alive.

The narrative format is, then, the genuine way of communicating within tribes, the "medium" of tribal consciousness. The world is explained via story-telling and is understood through these stories. There is as yet no difference between explaining and understanding. Every phenomenon that fits into the format of the narrative is accommodated therein. Open questions are included in the narrative and answered in it.

Tribal consciousness makes great use of the analogous mode of thought. There are no rigid, fixed contradictions but blurred boundaries between alike phenomena: the ancestors thought as their descendants think, and nature is like human life. Everything is connected, and a narrative can illustrate this. A fairytale, for instance, connects certain concrete problems with magical and amazing solutions from other dimensions of reality, which make one's own problem appear less insurmountable.

Rituals

Every community has its rituals, which involve symbolic actions (e.g. dance) and follow given rules. They serve to strengthen the spirit of community and balance the differences between individuals. They are also meant to sustain the tribe's harmony with its natural environment.

In a ritual, the community confirms its existence, creating in its members a sense of belonging and confidence. Rituals involve certain given processes and are mostly performed at fixed times. They cannot be changed at random or performed at another point in time. The ritual is an ahistorical, coincidence-free zone where things are the way they always have been.

The consistency and unchangeability of the ritual creates a sense of security in the face of the unpredictabilities of history.

This is how the ritual helps process fear. It gives rise to feelings of belonging and respect for tradition in a very unique way. It endows the otherwise linear history of man with an additional dimension of reliable recursiveness.

This idea will later be taken up for models of historical interpretation, such as Aristotle's circular causality, Friedrich Nietzsche's eternal return, or Oswald Spengler's concept of history.

Significantly, such models often come up at periods in history where rituals are losing power and influence.

Excursus: The Further History of the Ritual

Already at stage 2, there is a break with the ritual. Socrates was convicted for godlessness, probably because he ceased to take the prevalent customs of the Greek communities seriously, which was interpreted as a threat to the protection against the unpredictabilities of life.

With rituals losing their constitutive importance, the notion of coincidence gains more reputation. Ritual is a space free from coincidence and history. There, everything is just as it has always been.

This is how the quantitative principle works. It is in materialism that the power of the ritual is utterly broken. The numeric principle leads to the maximisation of the formal equality of all phenomena. While in one particular area this held benefits (equal rights before the law), in others it had grave consequences, which were connected with the fall of the ritual. For capitalist production, whose central idea is that of the maximation of profits, the value of every product is expressed in figures, namely in its price on the market. This value may change over time but is always apparent in the price. Suddenly, everything can be compared, not only apples with apples or refrigerators with refrigerators but even bicycles with wardrobes or victims of war on one side with victims on the other.

A ritual can only be compared to itself: Christmas is Christmas, a wedding is a wedding. When comparing one Christmas party with another, we always compare details: how much we ate, drank, laughed or sang, how many presents we gave away, or how much weight we gained. We cannot, however, compare them in terms of date or purpose.

The more we involve the principle of comparison in what we think or do, the more we become alienated from any notion of ritual. And the less familiar we are with our rituals, the more easily will we become exposed to the fears that the rituals would hold in their spell.

To the materialistic mind, then, everything is equal, like the basic components of matter, which bear no distinctive features. Society is organised accordingly, and ritual differences are eliminated. To equal measures, the seven days of the week are incorporated in the routine of business activities and consumption habits. The churches, the guardians of ritual, protest in vain against the levelling of the days of the week into seven equal periods. In sectors where Sunday is still invariably treated as a day off, the only reason for this is fear for people's regenerative capacities.

Another step in the undermining of rituals and their power was that of the universalisation of the characteristic processes of capitalist industrial production. Meaningless, minimalistically utilitarian rituals have become part of our everyday life. What does provide a minimum of ritual structure is habitual behaviour such as pushing the power-on button of the television set, indiscriminately using the car for locomotion, or purchasing ever more replaceable consumption goods. Such rituals of consumption provide a sense of reliability in uncertain and hectic times.

A ritual is not only a social act but also one of celebrating community. It requires the combined efforts of various people, heightening their sense of belonging. Therefore, every push of human consciousness towards individualism is made in opposition to ritualisation and may weaken its influence. We have mentioned Socrates, who was sentenced to death for seduction of youth. The seduction of youth he was accused of was in fact an act of leading his disciples out of the ritualised system of Greek tribal community. Philosophers formed their own groups with their own rituals, which were no longer grounded in the predominant tradition.

In materialism, another step towards solitariness is taken. Inanimate objects become more and more important to society, while the belief in human relations suffers. With the victory march of profit-oriented, rational thinking, even the realm of human relations is sooner or later searched for sources of quantifiable gain. With whom we spend time is now no longer just a question of enjoyment but also of measurable result. Relationships are a matter of free choice. The single man or woman of the age of materialism turns relationships on and off like the television. Other people are not just "there" as in traditional peasant families or tribal communities: they are contacted so they might meet certain needs. As soon as one object has been reached, we move on to the next activity. This is one of the reasons why rituals disappear in materialism. Individual rituals emerge to replace the abandoned ones, growing into obsessional neuroses and becoming the object of psychological examination and therapeutic treatment.

The personalistic stage, too, makes little of rituals. The principle of quantity may be despised, the power of figures may be contested, and the monotony of work may be detested, but the rituals are mistrusted for their nature of uniformity. The loner, whose looking for brilliance is often caught in the trap of narcissism, easily tires of any event proceeding in a uniform manner. Instead, he craves for the original and the unique, developing his own rituals to be able to alter them any time he wants to: he hates drifting along with the crowd. He prefers an adventure holiday on a tropical island to a traditional Christmas celebration.

Interestingly, rituals reappear at the systemic stage. Rituals (e.g. those of appreciation or presentation) perpetuate systemic processes. Although rituals are no longer understood as fixed or beyond dispute and can also be invented ad hoc, they cannot be introduced or altered single-handedly. As they are grounded in the social system they were invented in, they may easily be sustained by it. Gestures from days of old, such as bowing to the ancestors, are reintroduced in systemic Constellation work.

As the system cannot be directly manipulated by a single individual and every desire to lead always results in a new form of systemic integration, the individual has to resign himself to the fact that his role is restricted. With the system always one step ahead, defiant personalistic protest ("I will still have my way") will be to no avail.

The humility suggested by systemic thinking is enforced by rituals. The communities of this stage are chosen by their members rather than preordained by birth. In contrast to personalistic communities of choice, systemic ones have a holistic point of reference. (Systems point beyond their own matrix, requiring openness "towards the top level".) This point of reference helps stabilise the systemic community.

Finally, holistic consciousness reveals that rituals play an important part in the spiritualisation of everyday life. If simple or even annoying actions are performed in the spirit of the ritual, they become an act of celebration. It is not only Japanese-style tea drinking but also the traditional cleaning of cups that seems to become a special act.

Shamanism

"Shamanism" is an umbrella term for traditional spirituality and medicine in tribal communities. It contains social rituals, ceremonies of healing, and therapeutic treatments. One important aspect is the use of symbols, whose meaning is determined by the narrative tradition of a specific tribe. The cogency of these symbols lies in the faith of the community. Christian missionaries, for instance, who were strangers to a narrative community, could destroy one of its symbols without having to fear personal consequences; for members of the tribe it was a different thing. (St. Bonifatius, for instance, is said to have cut down an oak holy to the Chatti in the year 723, in an attempt to demonstrate the superiority of the Christian god to Germanic Donar.)

The fact that symbolic values are restricted to specific narrative communities allows for the conclusion that shamanistic exercises cannot simply be transposed into other contexts. That is why the application of such exercises in our modern day society with the aim to challenge habitual patterns, may have no outcome whatsoever or else lead to grievous psychological damage – especially if these exercises are accompanied with the consumption of psychoactive drugs. The impressive solidarity found within a tribe serves to level individual differences in the way stimuli are processed, so that when one of the members needs special help the others will notice and give it to him.

From other points of view, the materialistic one in particular, some of the shamanistic skills, such as the practice of curing by trance journeys, may appear astonishing or dubious. These methods have a healing power where man is still closely connected with nature or where the cord has not yet been cut. The shaman acquires and applies to his work the knowledge of nature. He, as it were, reads organic consciousness by falling back on its patterns of communication.

The pre-historic shaman has, however, a rather limited historical horizon, which does not go beyond the oral narratives of the history of his own tribe. His ideas are therefore very hard to explain to outsiders of the tribe; other narrative communities – and even more so people at other stages of consciousness – may easily misunderstand him.

Superstition

Traditional tales reveal the laws of nature. Nature is explained by people in the tribe through the medium of the narrative. Many of the explanations found in these narratives are now often referred to as superstitions. In the mythological framework of tribal tradition, however, these explanations have a meaning and an impact.

The term "superstition" helps define tribal forms of knowledge against, on the one hand, belief systems envisaging a being presiding over all nature (monotheistic views of God), and on the other hand, the transtribal explanatory models of the world of science. The term, however, does not justify the debasement of a specific mode of explanation but should be used to classify it as belonging to a certain level of experience.

At the tribal stage, there is no truth claim that exceeds the scope of tribal consciousness. This is the limitation that all modern tribal lore – as found in the esoteric scene of our day (new witches, soothsayers, etc.) and revived tribal traditions – has to bear with. On the other hand, structuralist research has revealed that there is actually no point in trying to impose modern ideas of reality on other forms of consciousness, thereby tearing down everything that is precious and meaningful to tribal communities. This would only be giving a sequel to the atrocities of former times, including the burning of witches and the persecution of heretics.

The influential idea of reincarnation belongs to the narrative reality of the tribal stage. The idea was embraced most significantly by the two eastern religions of Hinduism and Buddhism, while in the West it remained largely unknown well into the 19th century.

A past life, i.e. an earlier life of the soul in another body, can be imagined only through a narrative. It is impossible by definition to sensorially re-experience events of a past life, as the senses always relate to the present. Moreover, the body of the present life, with its very own sensory organs, is incapable of experiencing a body from an earlier time, even if it was once the abode of one's soul.

On the level of the narrative, however, these questions are irrelevant. Narrative interpretations work in relation to narrative communities. A myth creates a sense of community, and communities make sure of keeping the myth alive. Tales that are told again and again wield a strong influence on the inner metaphorical world. The closer a culture is to the tribal stage of consciousness, the more deeply will it be affected by its tales: take, for instance, Tibet, which due to its geographical position was until very recently spared the confrontation with the challenges of the stage of materialism.

Materialistic consciousness effectively subverts narrative traditions by installing, as it were, digital patterns of thought and causing a decline in analogous thinking. New fears, such as the fear of loneliness, can then no longer be exorcised by traditional tribal tales, because the primary source of power for these narratives is an indestructible community. If these communities are, however, split up, the tales only have an indirect, secondary power. (Think, for instance, of the extreme migratory movements of the past few centuries, which caused millions of people to lose reference to the constitutive context of their traditional tales, the country of their forefathers and its landscape). The connection with the source has effectively been cut.

The belief in past lives in the context of our modern Western society – as dominated by materialistic consciousness –, may indicate a yearning for the magical elements of a lost tribal culture. The cold rationality of the material world causes fear in some people. One possible reaction to this fear is that of adopting traditional beliefs from narrative communities that are either extinct or can be found only in very different contexts. The borrowed myth creates a sense of community and a meaningful tradition. This is how the teachings of reincarnation have earned their place in the enlightened world.

Our Tribal Roots

We know from systemic therapy and constellation work that our tribal soul holds a place for all blood-relations and that its memory reaches back several generations into the past. The need for togetherness is an essential aspect of our inner life. We need people who love us and whom we can love. Originally, this need is directed toward those that we have grown up with and that first gave us a place in life. Issues arising from those quarters touch us most deeply. New born babies not only know their parents but also have some idea of their grandparents, whether they are still alive or not, and even of their great-grandparents and great-great-grandparents. Adopted children "know" about their biological parents, and may search for them throughout their life. The toughest manager may be moved by the thought of an evening in Advent on grandmother's lap. The death of a close relative is what hits us the hardest. We share joy and pain with our closest relatives. Our connections with them are salient, unique.

We also know the desire to serve a certain purpose and to have a certain role in the community. We want to serve the whole. Friendships we look for and find in life are attempts to establish tribe-like connections and to once more feel a sense of belonging, equality, and common interest.

The wish of men to be respected by women and that of women to be respected by men causes a desire that perpetuates all sexual struggle. Deep inside we have always known how to respect the other sex.

Although rituals are on the wane in daily life, we still feel the power of celebrations and festivities and will again and again look for new forms for them. Also, we still enjoy stories; all kinds of fairy-tales and fantasy novels are popular today.

How can we find out what our heritage from the first stage of the evolution of consciousness is? Let us first consider what are the fears, fixations, and resources stemming from this stage of our past.

Characteristic Fears:

- the fear of being excluded (the drastic consequences of mobbing show how powerful this fear is)
- the fear of solitude, of growing up, and of being let down in relationships (corresponding experiences may put a severe strain on the psyche)
- the fear of magical powers (the "evil eye", black cats, Friday the 13th, etc.)
- the fear of being disloyal or selfish (whoever breaks the rules of the tribe risks expulsion from the community)

Negative Fixations:

- debasement of reason and rationality in favour of suspicions and fears
- fear of independence and assertiveness, of imposing one's will; consequently a tendency to allow oneself to be exploited or overcharged; proneness to manipulation where trustworthiness is; susceptibility to cults or cult-like groups promising a new social home
- belief in ghosts, supernatural powers, conspiracy, etc., debasement of and contempt for other groups (in-group versus out-group mentality)

Resources:

- trust in life, as nourished by the powerful relations in one's own family
- empathy for other people, understanding for their needs and burdens of the community
- a balance between giving and taking, a basic understanding of fairness

- healing encounters with nature
- priority of the community over the individual
- priority of children's needs over those of adults
- the importance of children's respect for adults
- the meaning of respect for one's elders

Exercises

The Ancestor's Exercise

purpose: fortification of one's position, raising one's trust in life

indications: uncertainty as to one's place in life, fear of the future

Instructions: Close your eyes and imagine your father and mother to stand behind you. (Usually the father stands on the right and the mother on the left, but this does not have to be so.) Now imagine your grandparents standing behind your parents. It is irrelevant if you met all four of your grandparents in person or not. Behind your grandparents, there are your great-grandparents. Again it is irrelevant if you know anyone from that generation or not, if you have heard about them or if you do not know anything about them at all. They do exist as your ancestors. Go even further in your imagination to the generation of your great-great-grandparents. Behind them, imagine an ever widening field of ancestors, stretching to infinity.

Out of this vast field of ancestors behind you, you now feel the power of life flowing into you, from both the paternal and the maternal side. The power of life is flowing together in yourself. Consciously inhale this power of your ancestors. It can help you to walk into the future with confidence and strength. Imagine now an important step you are going to take in your life, and be aware that you can take it with the power and the loving support of your ancestors.

This practice may help you take problems in life less seriously, because you feel the support of a power that will always be there for you and that is benevolent no matter what happens.

Moreover, your relationship with your parents, if you experience it as troubled, may improve. You will realise that your life was not simply given to you by your parents but that you stand in a long line of transmission, in which your parents are just one among many links.

The Circle Practice

purpose: strengthening of the sense of belonging

indications: fear of being excluded, feelings of loneliness and lack of contact

Instructions: Close your eyes and imagine sitting in a circle of people. Whether you know these people is not important. All you know is that you belong to this circle.

Slightly bend your arms to the outside, as if to touch the hands of those sitting next to you in the circle. Let the palm of your left hand point upwards and imagine that the person sitting to your left is gently laying his/her hand on top of it while you put your other hand on top of that of the person sitting to your right. Now imagine that through your left hand you breathe in the friendly energy of the person sitting to your left and of other members of the circle, that this energy flows into your heart and that you exhale it through your right hand, passing it on to the person sitting on your right. Say to yourself the following sentence: "I belong to the people that are disposed towards me."

This practice may help you feel that there will always be a place re served for you in the circle of mankind. Although you may have conflicts with people in your vicinity or where you work, on a deeper level all people are connected. In this circle of interconnection, everyone has his natural place.

Even if there is no one else around you and you long for someone's company, you needn't suffer from loneliness, because you can feel your connection with others, which exists even when no body contact is possible.

The Tree Exercise

purpose: to experience and make use of the hidden powers of nature

indication: worries, problems, powerlessness, isolation

Instructions: Walk out into nature and look for a tree that draws you near, that you want to move closer to. Get in contact with it: maybe you want to touch it, or lean on it ...

Feel the life in the tree, the energy flowing through it. This tree is an individual like you. It has a spirit of its own. Contact this spirit and speak to it.

This practice encourages respect for nature and its wonders. After all, you yourself are a very special miracle of nature. You can learn how to feel the elemental forces of nature and connect with them.

"Your" tree can be your confidant, to whom you can tell your sorrows and worries when you are not feeling understood by the people around you. Or you could visit "your" tree for recreation and in order to deepen a friendship.

These exercises are supposed to help you become aware of how far and how deep your roots reach back in time. These roots can lend you the same kind of strength that enabled prehistoric tribal cultures to survive and sustain their communities under difficult conditions. If you look at your life and its challenges in the awareness of this power, which is rooted in a powerful and close connection with nature, you will feel encouraged and supported.

* * *

The recollection of your tribal origin may also help you recognise and appreciate the fundamental significance of the first relationships of your life, established in the circle of the family you were born into. Whatever the circumstances of your family may have been: you yourself evolved from them, and the more of peaceful resources you can bring to them, the more of peace you will feel within.

Stage 2: Emancipatory Consciousness – The Human Quality of Individualisation

Good or bad, hero is hero.

(Francois de la Rochefoucauld)

Key aspects:
abandonment of tradition, individualisation, risk-taking, violence, emotions, power and rulership, fear of evanescence

Shibana is sitting in front of the hut watching the sunset. A toilsome day of work is over. Work has been especially arduous now that she is pregnant again. Her husband has been over at the longhouse within the last a few hours. They are discussing if, following the events of the last few days, it will be necessary to wage war again against the village beyond the hills or if they should ask the lord of the land for help.

There has long been no war. In front of the little altar with the figurines of clay in the corner of the hut, Shibana will daily thank the gods for the years of peace they have had. She hopes that the men's scorn would subside again, so that she and her children will be spared what she already experienced when she was very little. A horde of wild riders attacked the village. They all fled to the forest nearby, leaving their huts to be set on fire and their fields to be trampled. What followed was a long time of hunger and hardship, during which some of her siblings died. It would take years until they had enough again to pass through the winter without having to suffer from hunger.

She thinks of her children: she has given birth to many, and many of these have died at an early age. But two of them are about to come of age. And she fears for both of them, as there may be a war: for her son, who will have to fight, and for her daughter in case they should lose the war – then the enemy might attack the village.

* * *

Tom lays aside his guitar. There are a few coins in the case; he needs dope, but the money won't be enough. Since he left home, he has always been short of money. But he has his freedom. He can do whatever he likes. And once he has made it big music-wise, he will return, in a fat car, and his father will be dumbstruck. He will never again be able to order him around.

He will stay just a little, and then depart with a compassionate smile: once he feels nauseous from the smell of conventionality and confinement, he will just disappear and go back to the girl they all envy him for.

Abandoning the Traditions

After a very long phase of relative uniformity of social structures, which proved highly advantageous to the hunter-gatherers, the living conditions change with the neolithic "revolution" (starting around 10.000 – 8.000 BC). The invention of agriculture leads to sedentariness and the creation of individual wealth attached to landed property (property that cannot be transported and does not need to be consumed immediately but serves longer-term reproduction of life).

The protection of this property against potential robbers requires a new social system. There is consequently a task segregation between farmers and fighters, which causes a social divide with far-reaching consequences (slavery, feudalism, serfdom, etc.).

The new form of economy is in many ways still dominated by the tribal mentality but slowly waters it down. Working methods where individuals or smaller groups are on their own and work for individual advantage further the social differentiation and encourage the abandonment of the egalitarian social system of the tribal stage.

Another aspect is the move away from a direct integration in nature. In mixed farming (agriculture and livestock breeding), nature is tamed and made to serve human interests. Agrarian society depends on whether nature is successfully conquered ("Subdue the earth!"). It is the beginning of man's emancipation from the supremacy of nature, which will peak in its limitless exploitation as implemented by materialistic consciousness.

Although there are ceremonial sacrifices and official celebrations of nature supposed to balance the loss of complete intimacy with it (such as the harvest festival, which has remained popular to this day), it still has irrevocably been turned into an object. Nature is at first respected for this generous role. But the more people learn to bring nature and its forces under their control, their reverence fades. As soon as nature ceases to be threatening to man except in marginal areas, his respect for nature loses ground; and consequently, natural resources are unscrupulously exploited.

Dissociation from the Body

Man's dissociation from nature also includes his dissociation from his own body, which also happens in the aftermath of the invention of work by the agrarian society ("In the sweat of thy face shalt thou eat bread"). The body as part of nature is itself turned into an object of human purpose. It is to function for work. If the body refuses to cooperate, it is forced to do so. For the seeds must be sown and the harvest must be brought in, or else one will die of hunger in winter. The body's momentary needs are put last for the benefit of a plan it is supposed to go along with.

As man more and more emancipates himself from nature, the distance between people, too, increases. If we are less able to feel our own body, we will also find it less easy to feel for other people. Therefore, new principles for social relations start to appear, which are geared towards utility. Communities are no longer "naturally inevitable" units that just exist and to which each member belongs as a matter of course. They more and more depend on notions of utility: communities are expected to bring certain advantages, and if they don't, the individual may well do without them. Whenever necessary or convenient, people use other people as resources to meet their own personal ends. Herein lays the cause for the decrease of social solidarity and for the differentiation of the community into classes and castes.

The Emancipation of Sustenance

The idea of cultivating wild grasses and taming wild animals, thus acquiring some scope of planning and controlling life, may have sprung from the necessity of ensuring the survival of a growing population, in connection with the decreasing spatial possibilities for previous forms of economy. At the tribal stage, the power of tradition ensured the community's respect for nature. Now nature becomes a separate thing, the object of the schemes and intentions of the human race expanding its radius.

And so it is that between man and nature the sphere of products (i.e. nature modified by human hand) comes into being. With their "creations", people construct an intermediate world, which serves as the basis for the modern illusion of independence from nature.

What began with the invention of tools in the early phase of the evolution of the human race is now increasingly applied for the purpose of gaining mastery over nature. People bring in their cognitive faculties and open the perspective of the mechanisation of the world. A new feeling of power goes hand in glove with the revolutionary manner of production, as a consequence of the new feasibility.

Agricultural lifestyle requires the introduction of a linear concept of time, and by planning and controlling nature, man relativizes his dependence on natural cycles. The agrarian production of food requires planning for the future. For instance, a certain share of the harvest must be withheld as seeds for a later harvest season. The immediate fulfilment of one's needs must be postponed so that longer-term survival may be ensured.

Goal- and performance-oriented thinking evolve in people's heads, along with certain structures of evaluation, which are to motivate them to work harder by instilling the fear that their performance could not be enough to ensure their own survival. People can never work enough, there is always something more that could be done.

It is one of the typical human vicious circles: the pressure to ensure one's security causes greater insecurity, which is to be overcome by working even harder: this causes additional strain and greater insecurity. The source of known fears is shut down, only to be replaced by other species of fear. Such double bounds represent traps and formulae for individual despair, as portrayed in the myth of Sisyphus; at the same time, however, they represent a driving force of evolution.

Social Differentiation and Linear History

With the new class of specialised fighters not only the idea of legitimate violence is introduced but also the concept of the hero, who symbolises the abandonment of tribal tradition. The hero of the individualistic stage does not act according to traditional rules but to the requirements of the moment, accomplishing outstanding, unprecedented feats – like a soldier in the army who purposefully ignoring an order achieves a great victory. Homer defines the object of the hero: "Always to be the best and to stand out among the others." (This is the motto Peleus passes on to his son Achilles.)

With deeds standing out against the everyday actions of the "average person", the hero creates his own myths, bound to his actions and his name. Thus, he initiates his own tradition, which is independent from that of the tribe.

Thus, the individual steps out of the shadow of tribal anonymity and lays out the foundations for a new self-confidence. In the exuberance of this emancipative outburst, he celebrates his own unleashed will, flouts the rules of the group and breaks with its traditions. It is a self-confidence based on the idea of self-realisation and superiority over others.

A completely new concept of history evolves. The cyclic idea of history of tribal culture, with its rigid obligations to tradition is replaced with a view of history oriented at the outstanding deeds of individuals. History is beginning to be experienced as a linear, chronological structure with phases and eras, with a beginning and an end. The concept of fate enters the arena of consciousness: individual life represents a once-only chance that can be missed, and this single life is inevitably terminated by death.

The Genesis of the Hero

The dynamic of emancipation also causes the unleashing of emotions. It was the job of the tribe to regulate and curb strong emotions. Their cathartic realisation took place in the context of the ritual. Thus, individual needs and collective interests could be balanced on a regular basis.

The individual who has broken free from the confinements of tribal structures soon experiences unbridled surges of emotion. It is not rational thinking or planning that motivates man to depart for uncharted territory, rather a feeling of narrowness and limitation, along with the fear of missing "something", namely one's personal realisation and freedom.

The first word of the first known epic of European literature, the Iliad, is "wrath" (*menis*). It refers to the sense of power and overstepping of boundaries, the heat of emotions in which others are interpreted as a hindrance or a threat. Alexander the Great had already defeated his Persian enemies, and their king was dead. Others would have thought it fit at this point to rest and simply enjoy the power and glory that resulted from these achievements. He, however, lead his troops further into the east, under immense hardships, solely driven, as the historians claim, by a feeling of ardent longing (*pothos*).

Life within the tribe, in its very own perfection and elegance, brings with it certain limits to imagination, which the spirit of the emancipatory stage desires to or must transcend. The motivating factor for this is an unbridled emotional faculty. Intense emotional states are now frequently evoked via drug-taking. Drinking excesses are a rather typical characteristic of the emancipatory stage, and apparently every younger generation must tackle the issue of drugs and alcohol all over again.

Emotions enable the emancipated individual to experience his own authentic self and define it as independent of the tribal community and its customs. This is why he relies on his own feelings rather than tradition when making decisions. And should there be a lack of emotions, they are stirred via the consumption of certain substances.

In tribal culture, the exertion and distribution of power is strictly regulated. Who has got a say in what and who has the final word depends on the traditional rules of the tribe. Due to the limited size of the community, there are many democratic elements (and often our modern-day longing for democracy is attributable to the feeling of harmony one gets when in a community everybody gets a say and things are discussed until everybody is happy). The distribution of power between the sexes, too, is subject to traditional rules.

When emancipated man gains access to his own emotions, he exposes himself to his passions, and one of these is the passion for getting one's own way. The dynamic of power is unleashed and grows ever stronger in the indulgent pursuit of personal ends, even if this involves immoral actions. Eventually, intoxication by power may turn into savage frenzy over blood.

The force of man's obsession for power reflects in the fact that there have been very few people in powerful positions who were ready to give them up of their own accord – like Emperor Charles V. of Habsburg, who (partly for health reasons) transferred his reign at the age of 56 years and retreated to a monastery. Due to the incapability of the powerful to relinquish their power, another stage of consciousness becomes necessary at which the dynamics of power are curtailed.

The hero of individualistic consciousness strives for individual power by taking a course supported by no existing tradition whatsoever. He wants to shoot forwards, leaving behind all the traditional rules and customs.

His deeds are at first connected with the exertion of violence. He risks the destruction of the social balance, ignoring all rules and regulations in expanding his power. If the spreading of power is no longer checked, it will expand until it comes up against a limiting factor that cannot be overcome.

Every child tries this out in the first year of its life: the flat is creatively transformed or rather turned topsy-turvy until someone says that enough is enough. Every limit is fathomed out until it becomes plain what is possible and what is not.

The hero conquers, subdues, tears down, builds up, and rules, until he is dethroned. Power is exerted arbitarily and becomes an end in itself:

power for the sake of keeping and generating power. In principle, there is no limit to power; only, in real life, another power may set a limit. The increased exertion of violence for implementing power eventually leads to war.

With his insatiable hunger for power, the hero inclines towards unscrupulousness and cruelty. This is not a consequence of individual perversity or lack of character. From the viewpoint of individualistic consciousness, a hero can only be a hero if he is reckless. As long as he follows the tribal tradition, which rarely permits for individual arbitrariness, he will not make it as a hero in the individualistic sense. At the height of his power, he may show signs of generosity and clemency, which virtue was ascribed to many rulers in antiquity, often falsely so. These gestures, however, are not due to a rest of tribal ethos but represent a self-imposed limitation of power. The sovereign of the individualistic stage is beyond the notions of ethos, and no one can tell him what to do and what not.

The hero also founds new myths. His praise is sung in heroic epics. This may happen in an attempt at satisfying the deep-seated desire of tribal consciousness for social balance and limitation of power. However, in that they are intrinsically connected with individual names ("Gilgamesh Epic", "La Chanson de Roland", "Alexander Romance", etc.), the new myths infringe the tribal principle of equality. Therefore, guilt is subliminally woven into them. The narrative form of the heroic epic paves the way for the genre of the novel, which focusses on the psychological world of the individual (inter alia his feelings of guilt) rather than tribal traditional values.

For the individual obsessed with power must pay for his actions with guilt, which torments and plagues him at night. In the end, the mighty hero is alone, and there is no one who could free him from his guilt or comfort him in his waking moments of self-reflection.

Moreover, some time in his life the hero becomes acutely aware of the fact that he will not live forever; and all his brave deeds will seem futile in the face of inevitable death. In tribal communities, death could be integrated in a broader picture through rituals, where the survival of the tribe despite the death of one of its members was celebrated. The heroes of individualistic consciousness, however, fight alone and die alone. If an individual was thus powerful in life, the tragedy of his death is all the more keenly felt and must be repressed: which partly explains why the heroes of the myths are often gods or demigods rather than mortals. This is the origin of the long tradition of posthumously declaring heroes – or in our day, idols of pop music – as immortal. A legend of this stature must be enjoying an afterlife somewhere in a hidden realm, only to come back one day to perform more heroic deeds; or if not, he must at least be working miracles from out of his secret hiding place.

Patricide and the Origin of Patriarchy

One of the reasons for the hero's break with the tribe is his problematic detachment from his father, which is the theme of the famous tale of Oedipus. In many tribal cultures, the initiation of a young man corresponds with his stepping out of his position of dependence on his parents and results in his integration in the broader context of the tribe. Thus, the detachment from one's father and his authority is aided by the ritual. The young man becomes the subject of another authority, replacing loyalty to the father with loyalty to the tribe: thus, a boy becomes a man.

However, in the societies that replace the small nomadic communities of old, one's sense of belonging to a tribe is no longer firmly established. Due to man's sedentariness, the self-image of the tribe is reduced to that of a loose community of settlers. The feeling of unity within the tribe, which the constant companionship on endless wanderings helped sustain, can no longer be experienced, as the community is now scattered across a wide area of land.

Should the community take to wandering again, forced by warlike or economic pressure, the tribal sense of community is strengthened again. Longer-term sedentariness, however, tends to make tribal identity increasingly abstract. True community can be felt only through joint activity. The gradual abstraction of the notion of a shared identity foregrounds the development of more recent concepts of social identity such as affiliation to states or nations.

A counter-movement is revealed in the increasing interest in smaller communities. Attachment to the large group of the tribe is replaced with increased emotionalisation of the family community, which becomes tighter due to the new forms of accommodation. All members of the family share a single house, often for a lifetime. Notions of "home" and "family" become almost synonymous. Much later, when the decay of rural lifestyle sets in, these concepts are romantically projected onto the "greater days" of the past.

If the son wants to part with the father, he has to break out of this confinement. This may lead to conflict, not only because the father is losing a hand but also because he is obliged to surrender the power the tradition has granted him. The son has to symbolically kill his father and his loyalty to the family before he can walk into the world as an individual. The first heroic deed is then to withstand the father in direct confrontation, turn around and walk away, following one's own path into the thrill of the unknown. And as the father is abandoned, the tribal rules and customs are left behind as well. However, although the hero is now in a position of relative freedom, he is still obliged to introduce new laws and traditions to fill, as it were, vacancies.

A central cathartic theme in Greek tragedy is guilt, which torments the protagonist. One of the sources of this guilt, aside from that of the emancipation from nature, is the abandonment of the safe sphere of the tribe. This strikes at the roots of tribal consciousness, whose philosophy is that all members are part of a whole, which is made up of all these parts – no more and no less. If one part goes missing, the tribe must be redefined. Possible reasons for such a loss according to the tribe are death, marriage (exogamy), the foundation of a new tribe (e.g. for reasons of emigration), and excommunication. All these changes are supported with the rites of old.

It is not, however, envisaged that someone leave the tribe simply by his own choice, and there is no rite corresponding to this change. It is partly for this reason that in Greece tragedy evolves as a form of art at this stage, containing pronounced ritual elements supposed to provide a ritual framework for novelties of this kind. The subject material of ancient tragedies may derive from tradition, i.e. from aspects of tribal consciousness, but the revolutionary style and dynamic of the tale may be attributed to the emancipatory stage (take, for instance, the introduction of the stage dialogue by Aeschylus).

The individual who abandons the sphere of tribal unity and introduces a new tradition is plagued by feelings of profound insecurity. These lead to inner conflicts, which can no longer be processed by the strategies of tribal tradition but remain within. Man is alone with his guilt, like Oedipus, who as a blind man retreats to the desert, when the magnitude of his guilt becomes apparent. This ancient species of suffering is one of the reasons for the modern-day invention of psychology.

Another source of guilt lies in a fundamental change of the relationship between the two sexes. For securing the wealth accumulated by their sedentary lifestyle, the community relies on specialised warriors who are willing to use violence at any given time. With the social status of the warrior ever growing, the power-relations between men and women, which were relatively poised in traditional tribal communities, change in favour of men, whose physical advantages are now increasingly converted into social dominance. In almost all cases, the hero is a man, who makes use of his superior physical strength to perform his deeds.

The traditional tribe had to make sure of a balanced relationship between production and reproduction (resulting in most cases in a model example of ecological economy). Individual consciousness divorces these two areas. The reproductive, inner sphere is viewed as natural (= functioning in accordance with nature), less interesting, and less important (= still functioning along the lines of the remnants of tribal consciousness). The new and revolutionary, the exciting and intense, on the other hand, happens on the periphery, where there is war and conquest – and where men are active.

Women are thus removed from the sphere of power. The active energy having passed from the centre to the periphery (the frontier is pushed further and further back), women are left behind in the centre. Reproduction is devalued in favour of production (of power).

Women are so affected by this change that they will frequently use all their creativity for reproduction. For a very long time, therefore, examples for female creative activity beyond reproduction will be a rarity, mostly found in women who have been exempted from the reproductive sector (as in the temple schools of antiquity or in medieval convents). The creative activity of the individualistic stage, with its groundbreaking artistic and scientific achievements, was almost exclusively a male domain. The imbalance between the centre and the periphery, which enabled the blossoming of the individual, was from the beginning connected with a predominance of masculinity. Recklessness and cruelty are no aspects of the feminine archetype; reproduction is possible only if the offspring is treated with love and care, and the responsibility of cultivating, developing, and passing on these energies is left wholly to women.

This fundamental change in attitude had a lasting influence that can still be felt today. However, it has to be said that men did not seize power for mere maliciousness or genetic make-up. They simply thought themselves obliged to make use of that in which they excelled women, their physical strength, to ensure their survival in the context of a new economic and social order. At times of scarcity of resources, they sought to protect and defend their economic surplus by means of physical violence and armed force. In the average case, men are simply more suitable for this job than women.

Often women in families increase their loss of power by feeling inferior, a feeling they pass on to their daughters. Female exertion of power is then restricted to the domestic sphere and is frequently made impossible even there. The relation between the sexes is locked into a rigid allocation of roles, where women have less influence and fewer rights, which is then increasingly converted into stereotypical debasement of their qualities: "Women are less intelligent, virtuous, and reliable than men."

The Invention of Polarity

Pythagoras attributed the even, light, and correct to man, while the uneven, dark, and false were ascribed to woman. This classification shows that with the confinement of woman to the depoliticized inner sphere, polar, dual thinking is introduced also. Thinking in nuances is on the wane, while thinking in oppositions grows ever in popularity, providing the prerequisites for the digitalisation of the world, whose beginning is the invention of science.

However dominant men may be at this stage of consciousness, we should bear in mind that all the relevant steps of evolution are taken by the culture as a whole; women's part in them is just as important. They, too, yearn to break out of the tribal structure. However, since in its beginnings this stage places such a great emphasis on fighting skills and outward expansion, women are forced to stick to the sphere of the polar opposite of domestic peacefulness and reproduction. Various cultural patterns are then developed, which will make the role of woman appear as set in stone.

While men are able to participate in and benefit from the enormous developments that this and succeeding stages bring, the role of the woman in society remains persistently fixed through the ages, until, at last, at the personalistic stage the contradiction becomes too obvious to further be ignored, and a movement of female emancipation is born.

The male protagonists of the second stage of consciousness have to suppress their fear of losing their tribal roots and the grounds of their existence. They monopolise all forward movement in human development. All that is left to women is then the retrospective respect for ancient lore and values. It is not before materialistic consciousness comes up against impenetrable limits that genuine female strength is really appreciated. At around this time women start to actively get involved in the process of the development of consciousness. Within a short time, they have to retrace the steps of a path of evolution that men walked before them. That this is unsettling to men is not wholly surprising.

The Power of the Intellect: Heroes of the Mind

The relativisation of tribal tradition has other far-reaching consequences, which already become apparent in the advanced civilisations of antiquity with their sophisticated division of labour, advanced techniques of administration and the scientific findings made possible by all this. As surplus products of the organisation of a new social system, these cultural achievements help establish a new dimension of emancipation – emancipation that is not based on power or violence but represents a new form of peaceful coexistence.

In Greek antiquity, an enormous breakthrough of individual achievements takes place, and within a relatively short space of time an abundance of new ideas is conceived and documented. Greek intellectuals also use their sophisticated written culture to record the names of the great minds, the heroes of Apollonian consciousness.

Tradition appears in a new guise and is given a different status once the step from oral to written tradition is taken. The myths are written down and thus established. The authorities of tradition are no longer the narrators – that is, the elders of the tribe – but those who can write.

Intellectuality is then a new power and a polar opposite to the power of the armed man. The "heroes of the mind", the adventurers of the intellect, are just as fascinating as the explorers. They display an unprecedented abundance of creativity, as if individuality, suppressed over thousands of years by tribal consciousness, had finally broken free from its shackles.

A particular type of emancipatory individualism is that of the founders of a religion or teachers of spiritual wisdom. They are portrayed as people with outstanding abilities or eccentric personality traits (often they display skills bordering on tribal shamanism to demonstrate their extraordinary abilities). At a certain point in their lives, they broke out of the confines of the predominant social order and started to follow their own paths, like Prince Siddharta, who abandoned his predestined career as successor to the throne, or Jesus of Nazareth, to whom early on the scholars of the temple were more important than his parents.

Courageously abandoning their habitual patterns and their social securities, they finally experience a radical transformation. Revealing themselves as individuals with insights into universalistic consciousness, they are adored by some and hated by others.

In the path of reformation, they have pointed out the solution to individualistic consciousness. The actual courage of a hero lies not in the conquering of dangers and the slaying of monsters but in breaking with all traditions and entering new territories of consciousness. The fears that limit individuals in their actions at the tribal stage must be excorsised, and this requires a great deal of heroic courage. There is fear of loneliness, fear of the unknown, fear of the forces of nature, and fear of the abyss of emotions.

Overcoming these fears does not call for violence and brutality, nor does it require recklessness or blind egotism; what is required is readiness to leave one's safe, habitual environment to endure the twists and shocks of the unknown. The heroes of the mind, then, venture to the edge of familiarity to have a greater vision.

The heroes of brute force, too, basically seek for the borders of consciousness, but all they encounter is death and burnt down villages. It is only on the day they die that they actually find the borders of consciousness, but they can tell no one about it. Yet among posterity there are always some who will glorify these senseless deaths.

The discrepancy between the ambitions of the adventurers of the sword and those of the adventurers of the mind reflects in Diogenes's ridicule of Alexander, who is totally ignorant of what the mocker is trying to tell him.

This is how we might interpret Socrates's statement (according to Plato) that philosophising is learning to die, i.e. radically departing from one's habitual ways of thinking and feeling, even though they will cease to ensure inner safety. A philosopher with a spiritual goal is ready to sacrifice everything that promises reliability in life in order to experience the Universal and surrender to it, for better or for worse. Socrates himself set an example with his death.

The fearlessness of the seeker of the truth enables him to break with the egotism of individualism. Whatever they find at the borders of perception they share with other people, so that they may lead a better life and experience inner growth. Thus, they serve the cause of the development of consciousness, ensuring that the spark of liberation, the spark of holistic consciousness not only survives but is kindled in as many souls as possible. This explains the missionary zeal of those who have found the truth. They greatly differ in their communicative talent of telling people still caught up in their tribal or existential fears their insights without instilling more fear in them but making them feel understood.

As the teachers of wisdom are blessed with special gifts and great courage, they can reach the highest levels of consciousness. They frequently display great optimism in view of liberation from suffering and of universal salvation, heaven on earth or the end of reincarnations – saying that the complete transformation of the world will not be long in coming, that it is just around the corner.

In fact, the Jews have been waiting for the coming of the Messiah to this day, and the Boddhisattva, who cannot attain full enlightenment before all feeling creatures are freed from suffering, still has a lot to do.

Today we may presume that mankind must in one way or the other go through all the stages of consciousness before the fulfilment of religious prophecies about a realm of peace can become reality, and that this process will take a long, long time. The model of consciousness supports the idea that the process is headed irreversibly in the direction of the final goal of liberation, and that it makes sense to let one's own activities and aspirations serve this development, so as to diminish human fear. With regard to the millions of years that mankind has been evolving, the question when the kingdom of God on Earth will come is not that important. What is more important is the question whether we trust that the entire human life and the innermost core of every individual aspires to this goal and urges into its direction.

Our Emancipatory Roots

Every new generation questions and wants to reform the established values. Every young person must face the challenge of shaping his own identity and distinguishing himself from others and the norms of society. These are the roots of emancipatory motives. The prevalent norms are experienced as a limitation to individual and collective freedom and are seen in opposition to the evolution of mankind and the creation of new opportunities.

The conflict between conformity and rebellion is the basic pattern for many social and psychological conflicts. It plays a certain role in all the important steps in life. For human life to exist, an ovum must separate from the complex of all the cells in an ovary and embark on a solitary journey. Later the sperm cell separates from the mass of other spermatozoa to fertilize the ovum. Birth is another big step. The security of the mother's womb, the life of symbiotic coexistence with the maternal organism, is left behind and an independent individual is born. During the second year of its life, the child's intimate bond to its mother is somewhat loosened and it independently explores the world. The next big step involving emancipatory consciousness is taken in puberty with the distancing from one's family.

We know the tension between adventure and security, which urges us to leave behind the familiar and comfortable to take risks. Many of our actions are motivated by a desire for greater freedom. If we have for a while been living with certain structures, we will yearn for change and reform. Whenever we manage to take such a step we feel liberated.

Let us now focus on the characteristic imprint on our inner life of phase two of the evolution of consciousness.

Characteristic Fears:

- fear of losing love and affection while pursuing one's own interests (others love me only if I am the way they want me to be)

- fear of making the wrong decision (every wrong decision diminishes individual opportunities and prospects for personal freedom)
- fear of "getting a raw deal", of missing something (life is short and time should not be wasted)
- fear of irreversibility and finality (with every step I leave behind securities and the certainty that I can return to where I was before)
- fear of revenge (every risky step may limit other people in their freedom, who may then make plans of paying me back in the same coin)
- fear of personal inadequacies (if I am too cowardly, too unimaginative or too convenient to break through personal boundaries, nothing will become of me)
- fear of death (death puts an end to the pursuit of power and emancipation)

Negative Fixations:

- restlessness and "drivenness" (the unsteady mind)
- discontent with the present state of affairs, contempt for tradition, fixation on the future, idealisation of any innovation (the restless revolutionary)
- inclination towards exaggeration and egomania (the boaster)
- inclination towards excessive and addictive behaviour (the unrestrained daredevil)
- holding on to pubescent defiant behaviour (the opposer in principle)

Resources:

- self-confidence, confidence in one's own scope, abilities, and talents
- respect for people's individuality and uniqueness
- courage and commitment, willingness to help
- acknowledgement and maintenance of one's own interests
- love of innovation and exploration, creativity

Exercises

The Energy of the Transition to Adulthood

purpose: awakening that potential which is first set free at the time of the transition from adolescence to adulthood

indications: fear of one's own power, lack of courage, helplessness

Instructions: Look back on the time of your puberty: what were your dreams, what values or ideals did you cherish? What is your attitude towards them now? Which of these values still hold for you, which ones have changed and why?

While you think about all this, allow the feelings to arise in you that you had in that episode of your life. How do these feelings manifest in your body? Are they pleasant or unpleasant? Are there feelings that could help you in your present situation? How could the forces of that time support you in the face of present challenges?

This exercise can help you reconnect with the energy you used in your adolescence. You may remember this time as a difficult period in your life, but frequently such difficulties came up in connection with your inability to fulfil your desires. Maybe now, at this time of your life, you want to live the dreams of your youth?

The Departure

purpose: strengthening one's power for renewal

indications: fear of change, tendencies to sustain what is no longer beneficial

Instructions: Think about the departures in your life: times when you left behind the familiar and the convenient for pastures new. What was the driving force behind this? What pushed you off, what drew you near? What were you impatient to leave behind, where were you trying to go? What did you learn during the journey? What do new departures mean to you now? Are you happy with your life, or do you want it to change? Is there anything about your present situation that should change? Is there anything you want to leave behind, and if yes, where would you go to? There may be feelings or habits you want to change. Relax and concentrate on your own self. Let images arise before your mind's eye, images of your wishes and desires. Do not censor or reduce these images but marvel at what your soul is showing you.

This exercise may help build your confidence that you can plan your life according to your own ideas, that you can change what has begun to go wrong, and integrate what you approve of. You may realise that your life has greater potential than you thought it has.

Challenges

purpose: learning to see problem areas in one's life as challenges

indications: difficulty in handling innovation or change; a tendency to avoid confrontation and evade difficult situations

Instructions: Every stage of life has its challenges. What are the challenges you are facing in your present life – in relationships with other people, at work, or regarding the cultural or political dimension? What resources will it take for you to rise to these challenges? Close your eyes and think of a difficult situation in the past that you mastered well. Try to remember the inner strengths and positive qualities that availed you then. How could you use them in dealing with today's challenges?

This exercise may help you take on difficult situations with confidence and use your resources to improve these situations.

* * *

These exercises may help develop the hero/the heroine within. In your life there are situations where you must force yourself to do something. If you connect with the energy of this stage, you will find it easier to take heart and accept the challenge. You will enjoy to try out new things and set out for new adventures. And you will learn to creatively deal with difficult situations.

Stage 3: Bureaucratic Consciousness – Human Life in Organisations

The best leaders are those their people hardly know exist. The next best is a leader who is loved and praised. Next comes the one who is feared. The worst one is the leader that is despised.

(Lao Tzu, Tao Te King)

Key aspects:
administration of rulership and curtailment of arbitrariness, rules and norms, security, dependence, control of emotions by shame, fear of chaos

Everything was strictly regulated. The style of the first character, the form the individual characters had to have, even the dipping of the goose-quill into the ink followed a preset order. Every day after breakfast, Brother Anthony would sit down at his workplace and write character after character interrupted by the ritual prayers and by meals. For two years had he been copying the New Testament, thanking God for the work He gave him.

For well he knew that he was never safe from the temptations of the devil; but whenever he had let his mind wander off and found emotions that he could not approve of, he would retreat to his father confessor, who would help him clear it up before God.

Brother Ambrosius entered the room. Rumour had it that he was chosen to be the successor of the abbot. Would he then be put in charge of the scriptorium? He scolded himself inwardly. Instead of nursing dreams and wishes, he should go about his scriptorial work with diligence and devoutness. Every unnecessary and especially every selfish thought could detract from the exactitude and beauty required of his work.

***

After more than a hundred applications, Martina has finally received an invitation to a job interview. She is well prepared: she carefully considered what to wear, did her research on the firm and practised the things she would say in reply to standard questions. After dreary months of waiting, she longs for a permanent job that will provide her life with structure and for which she will be paid regularly. Therefore, she must be especially careful to do everything right. She is excited and hopes that she will make no mistakes at the interview.

She wants to be one of those who will get a decent fee and can afford a certain standard of affluence. That could then provide the basis for a small family – though of course the right man has yet to be found.

The Necessity of Order

When the Visigoths took Rome in the year 410 AD under their king Alarich, they hit the Romans very hard, leaving a trail of destruction. However, after three days' sacking they withdrew from the city because they did not quite know what to do with it. They had no idea how to govern a city of that size. When In 2003 the US and their allies took over Iraq ... – we know the rest.

A territory once conquered must be governed also, but this is not of interest to the storyteller who sides with the hero rather than the bureaucrat. After all, what could one say about the compiling of lists and the handling of figures, about the logistics of providing thousands of people with food? However, the skills of the officials are asked for whenever after a successful invasion the conquered territory must be administered to ensure long-term profit.

For this purpose, a new human type emerges. For the bureaucrat to come into being, the individual must first emancipate and isolate himself (stage two of the evolution of consciousness). Tribal structures must have dissolved before a hierarchy of officials can be established. Officials must be loyal to their sovereign, not to their tribal group of descent.

The phenomenon of corruption is one of the major problems of bureaucracy. It occurs whenever on the level of external action tribal bonds have been dissolved only superficially, where there has been a rather unstable deconstruction of tribal attitudes. Every official tends to neglect the norms he is to keep to if human relations important to him happen to enter into his area of responsibility.

At this stage of consciousness, emotions are reined back considerably. The subject must restrain himself and to conform to the social norms. It is made clear to him that if he does not do so he will lose not only his job but also his life. Even the sovereign himself must keep a tight rein on himself, as it is his job to ensure the reliability and stability of the state system and act as guarantor for it. Both spiritually and physically, he represents the holy order of his kingdom and must act accordingly.

Who would envy a dictator who has to stoically watch the troops on parade for hours on end? Such absurd demonstrations of power are regularly engineered: they serve to lock together the ruler and his subjects. These strict rituals no longer serve the cause of overcoming basic threats to survival but that of protecting bureaucratic power. The state becomes God, and, to equal measures, the ruler and the subject serve its interests, expressing their membership to this system by obeying and conforming to it.

In the course of history there have been countless forms of interaction between stage two and stage three. One example for this is the dynamic between centre and periphery. In places where a hierarchical government has been established, wealth is accumulated, which on the basis of a monopolisation of power leads to a blossoming of craftsmanship and trade. This new wealth provokes the "wild" tribal braves at the periphery of the state system into demanding their share. The consequence is robbery and plunder at the periphery or, in some cases, pushes into the very centre of wealth and administration. We have mentioned the Visigoths, who managed to take Rome in 410; other examples include the Vikings and the Magyars in the 9th, the Mongols in the 13th, and Al Qaida in the 21st centuries.

The hierarchical system, which is at first too inflexible to tackle the problem, is destabilized by the invaders. There are then two basic possibilities: either the invaders actually take over power and introduce a new hierarchy, or the endangered state system successfully resists. In the long run at least, the strategy of selective destruction and plunder makes no sense, as it gradually undermines its own basis. Sooner or later there will be nothing left to plunder (this is why even the Thirty Years' War had to end). If the infrastructure has been ruined completely, the economy will break down and the plunderers will be left with their treasures. In some cases, the plunderers of stage two, having reached the dead-end to their strategy of "vandalism", catch up with stage three in order to enjoy its cultural benefits.

The Bureaucratisation of Individuals

Even the spiritual and intellectual breakthroughs that began at the stage of individualisation are institutionalised. If a religious movement centred around its founder is to become a Church, i.e. if the new ideas and the spiritual message are to be enshrined in tradition, bureaucratic steps must be taken. If a scientific finding is to inspire a new world view, it must be documented, discussed, and verified by the scientific community, which would never function without certain bureaucratic elements.

Emancipatory consciousness invented war, for which a military apparatus is developed. From the latter, the principles of bureaucratic systems are deducted. Fixed chains of command, defined by irreversible and permanent relations of super- and subordination, form the basic structure of bureaucratic organisations. Complementary (top-bottom) relations become the defining element of the new social order and orientation. Through rankings, every member of the community is allotted a station it must not leave. These stations are determined primarily by birth and thus not subject to individual manipulation. The destiny of descent is inevitable.

The hierarchical stage involves the taming of despotism, which eventually destabilises and breaks individualistic consciousness. If [find original version] (as Thomas Hobbes uses the metaphor of the wolf) – that is, if individual demand for power meets individual demand for power –, the fight will continue until the enemy is broken and eliminated. And every victor must face new opponents, who are jealous of his success, and often the most revered warrior suffers the most horrible death.

This chain of warlike heroic deeds (which in medieval Europe or in Japan caused the extinction of entire aristocratic clans and a drastic reduction of the living expectancy within the warrior caste) must be broken. A superordinate structure is introduced, which subdues the violent individualist: the state.

The foundation of states is both a consequence of individual arbitrariness and a remedy against it, as the aim of the conqueror is to firmly establish his power. The law must step in the place of wilful action.

The introduction of the law frequently involves the application of tribal strategies. Laws are said to be of "divine" origin, just as the rules of tribal communities are legitimised by a tradition the individual cannot change. Even the actions of the powerful sovereign, which are still not free from arbitrariness, are subject to divine judgement.

The state claims for itself the monopoly on the use of force. This development already took place in the ancient Egyptian realm and, in the preceding course of history, is again and again challenged and set back by the individualistic principle; basically, U.S.-American society has not solved the problem to this day for its insistence on the right of individuals to bear arms). Every form of violence is legally regulated and limited.

The individual must restrain his anger and aggression, lest he experience the full force of even greater aggressions. Emotions can no longer be expressed at will but are subject to social rules and regulations. One indication for this cultural leap is that of the spreading of the concept of medieval courtly love, meant to instil "higher" values in the murderous and devastating knights. Instead of the craft of destruction they should learn the principles of "courteous chivalry". Aspirations to power are inhibited via the instilment of aspirations to prestige, reputation, and status.

A hierarchical society tends to apply mechanisms of conditioning to motivate or force the subjects to behave according to norm. Legally imposed systems of reward and punishment are meant to make people repress their emotional impulses and become well-behaved citizens whose actions are predictable and reliable.

Drastic corporal punishment as a deterrent indicates the power the state wields over the individual, instilling in him the fear of infringing the laws. Most societies in the modern era have abandoned all forms of physical penalty and have been developing ever more differentiated systems of punishment oriented at the principles of materialistic consciousness. However, the increasing complexity of these societies necessitates the introduction of additional sets of rules and regulations as well as institutions of control.

Every attempt at establishing standardised behavioural patterns is experienced as pressure by the individual and creates resistance. People long to escape the bureaucratic control and observation, looking for every imaginable way out of it. The result is a social spiral effect or cat-and-mouse game: authorial control causes the people to turn to loopholes and dodges, and improved control causes them to look for other tricks and back doors.

Norming by Shame

As an inner regulatory element for the standardisation of individuals, shame is institutionalised. The root of shame goes back to the tribal stage. Its function within the tribe is to inform its members of having violated a social rule, so that they may change direction and reintegrate into community.

Importantly, these physical reactions happen automatically and without the involvement of thought. Social rules are indoctrinated on a deep emotional as well as physical level so that they can no longer be questioned. Frequently it is religion that mediates the social rules and standards, providing additional security for their internalisation by its own means.

Very clear examples for the creation of social conformity by shame can be found in East Asian cultures, where suicide is still sometimes committed for only trifling rule infringements. Apparently, "losing face" and having to live in disgrace seems a fate literally worse than death. If an individual can go as far as to kill "aberrant" members of his own family under the pretext of removing collective disgrace, then this only goes to show how utterly successful has been the subjugation of the people to the interests of a state or a religion.

The Institutionalisation of Violence

As the state gradually gains control over the individual, its power increases; and institutions are created to administer this power. Bureaucracy is invented, along with the archetype of the official. He, in contrast to the slave to the state, is a freeman, although his actions are bound by governmental directives. He acts as right-hand person of the state. For this he is compensated with money and goods and lent a certain amount of prestige, which increases in proportion to the success of the hierarchical system. (In the late Roman Empire, for instance, many officials started out as slaves, gained their personal freedom thanks to the prestige of their bureaucratic occupation and frequently rose to great power.)

The scope of arbitrary individual action becomes increasingly narrow. Risings of the nobility mark the resistance against this trend; the rivalry of two opposing systems continues for centuries, filling history and fiction books alike.

Moreover, on an international level, states retain the principle of arbitrariness from the individualistic stage. Against other states, wars are waged, feuds are carried on, and there is blackmail, robbery, rape, and murder. The introduction of international law may be regarded as a logical step away from this form of anarchy; however, it has been impossible to this day to provide this legal system with a monopoly on force that would step in to stop the frenzy of individual states. The international community is still undecided as to the question whether states should be subordinated to a global system, as individual nations remain adamant about their right to state-based arbitrariness. Among themselves, states often appear as rowdy adolescents who sneer at the law and defy or ignore their authorities. Their irresponsibility is paid for by the countless victims of military and structural violence.

In the future, however, the introduction of a supranational monopoly on force must inevitably follow. Posterity will look back in horror upon our age, just as we might look upon the violence of the middle ages or the slavery of Roman antiquity. How long the power of national egotism will be in decreasing will probably depend on the readiness in individuals or groups of people to recognise and resolve the harmful aspects of their own egotism.

Violence is done on all levels of hierarchical organisations. There are the continuing acts of war on the international level, but there is also a great deal of violence within – in education, in business, and, "of course", in the military. For a long time, it was assumed that children had to be beaten to learn the rules of conduct and morality. Novels by Charles Dickens bear testimony to this. In the early days of industrialisation, a factory owner was allowed to inflict corporal punishment on his employees, and at school in our part of the world this kind of treatment was officially permitted up until a few decades ago. Many people, including high clerical dignitaries, still entertain the thought that there is such a thing as a "healthy" box on the ears. They justify their position with a conviction beaten into them that the only way they could have become upright servants of the bureaucratic establishment was through the brutalities they themselves were subject to. Talk of a "a good thrashing that someone deserves" reflects the intimate and perverse alliance of violence and the system.

The most effective way of becoming oblivious to one's own mental torment is to inflict the same kind of suffering on others. Therefore, former victims of authorial violence tend to justify their maltreatment and often become violent themselves.

Thus, domestic violence is handed down from generation to generation, fulfilling the role of some inadequate putty that keeps the edifice of the system from collapsing. It is a mixture of fear and suppressed agony, which bends and breaks the people, until they deny and forget their own will.

Thus, through violent measures, the hierarchical system encourages more violence, which it then attempts to check by all means available. This is one of the major dilemmas of this stage, which again and again causes hierarchical consciousness to come up against its limiting factors.

World Religions

There is a strong connection between the hierarchical stage and world religions. Although the phenomenon of religiosity already features as a salient element in tribal cultures, the large-scale spreading of one single creed is not possible at stage one. Every tribe develops its own religion, which is strongly linked with the natural environment. As such a religion is usually connected with the founding myth of the respective tribe, it cannot be transferred to other tribes.

However, as people cluster into larger groups as a consequence of the Neolithic Revolution, and as they found states which come to accommodate people in unprecedented concentrations in the city areas, religions evolve that lay claim to apply to several tribes (e.g. Judaism) or, later, the entire human race (e.g. Christianity, Islam).

Thus, as soon as the idea of universality as connected with individualistic expansion (i.e. the idea of the empire) has entered human consciousness, there is also a demand for a universal system of values that will hold the population of a vast area of conquered land together.

Another important element of these complex organisations is the increased use of written language. The world religions take profit from this development. They no longer have to rely solely on the oral medium to spread their message but have the opportunity to reach many people via written language. The written medium in turn becomes associated with the hierarchical authority, so that everything in writing is highly respected.

Written language makes it possible that the fame of the founders of religions spreads all over the world and that their message is kept alive through the ages. Impressive religious personalities may have been before writing, but their following must have been restricted because they lacked the tools for spreading their message.

In the thousand years from 500 B.C. to 500 A.D. in particular, various people appear as preachers and prophets, whose deeds and ideas are recorded in writing and whose messages gain supra regional importance. Many of these have indeed reached the highest level of consciousness and found a way of communicating their spiritual insights to contemporaries so as to let them experience a significant expansion of their own mind. Typically, it is the disciples that record the teachings of their masters, which frequently leads to misinterpretations. (Had St. Paul not passed his master's message on to the goys, with certain changes he thought fit, then perhaps Jesus would have remained no more than a Jewish rabbi or prophet.) The disciples pass on the teachings, which are finally canonised, i.e. written down in a form defined as unchangeable. However, the disciples have often not reached the high plane of consciousness of their master's and will consequently distort the basics of his teaching by applying inadequate strategies from the lower stages of evolution to communicate them.

The hierarchical stage of consciousness (hierarchy = holy order) provides the ideal framework for the spreading of new religions. Various religions benefit from the infrastructure, which was initially developed for administrative and economic purposes. Not only commercial products but also religious messages travel overland by the good roads of commerce.

While many new religions start as individualistic revolutionary movements and are opposed by the establishment (this is why some people regard Jesus as a freedom fighter), they will often end up being instrumentalised by the representatives of the system of state. Once the teachings have been canonised (i.e. their official version has been put out) and a hierarchical structure has been established within the religious community, the process of the integration of religion into the worldly hierarchy can begin. The immense accumulation of power by the bureaucratic apparatus is justified by alleging that its major authority, the sovereign, directly descends from the highest being.

This is how religion enters into the sphere of power, which inevitably corrupts its universalistic purport. It is particularly the monotheistic religions that are in danger of developing in that sort of direction, as in their view of God the hierarchical model is reflected or can easily be reflected.

To many theological theorists, Christianity loses its liberating force due to the Constantinian shift and its rise to a state church, whereby it turns from opposing worldly authority to representing worldly authority itself. The heretics of the middle-ages, who again and again demand for a disempowered church, voice the discontent of many believers with a religion gone bureaucratic.

On the other hand, the accumulation of worldly power by the state is kept in check by the proponents of religions. The values of humanity are preached to despotic leaders and their acolytes. In many ways, the church acts as protector of the weak and the wronged. The admonitory power of Western religion paves the way for the implementation of human rights, partly because on the basis of imperial structures it can lay claim to universality. Everyone should believe and be converted to religious faith. The abovementioned decision St. Paul made in the early days of Christianity is significant also in the following sense: a God is preached who does not belong to a single people (such as Yahwe, the God of the Israelites) but wants to bring salvation to everyone in the world, no matter what tribe they are descended from.

The Domination of Nature

Nature is regarded by the bureaucratic system as something of an adverse opposite. It represents all the unbureaucratic qualities: uncontrollability, unpredictability, and chaos.

As a sign of superiority to nature, the bureaucratic ruler erects monumental buildings, which he places in nature as if to besiege an enemy. Then he confines domesticated nature within: in his palace he takes pleasure in pruned trees and tamed beasts. The triumph over the forces of nature is achieved by exerting violence. Outside the palaces, roads and channels are built regardless of the natural realities. Through the building of dams and irrigation systems, nature is made to serve the growing population.

In this cause, too, the ruler is backed by religion, insofar as it is a faith proclaiming a higher being superior to the forces of nature. This is why for a long time the proponents of religion rather than those of the sciences have the sovereignty of interpretation of nature and its forces. If there is a natural disaster, the priest, not the scientist, is asked to give an explanation.

Creativity at the Bureaucratic Stage

At this stage, creativity is caught up in the basic dilemma of the hierarchical/bureaucratic paradigm: the system demands for permanence, which the strict regulation of life is to ensure. The only time creativity is asked for by the establishment at this stage is when it is looking for new strategies to perfect its control over the people. Under conditions of rigorous control, however, it tends to waste away. Only in a place of freedom can it grow. If a bureaucratic system fails to find creative answers to change, it may collapse quite abruptly, as was the fate of planned economies around 1990. On the other hand, if creativity is given too much scope, bureaucracy is threatened.

If people want to lead an organised life, very large and complex communities can hardly do without bureaucracy. In order to feel content, however, they need to allow for the development of their creativity as well. This is why for every form of hierarchical control the establishment comes up with there is a counter-movement. The more rigorous the control is that the state exerts, the more loopholes are discovered, from silent refusal to the telling of jokes as a medium of resistance.

In hierarchical systems, art is often created as a means for securing bureaucratic power (panegyric poetry and decorative music at court for the purpose of incensing or glossing over the sovereign's exercise of power). However, there is also a leaning among many artists under the bureaucratic rule towards subversiveness (underground poetry, rebellious painters, derisive composers). Rebellious art is fought by all means available, and its central theme is protest against this oppression. Most of the art of this epoch is thus in one way or the other dependent on the bureaucratic system, either glorifying or criticising it. However, there is still some art that is not dependent. Like a signpost, the creative "surplus", which turns art into "good" art, points out the path towards overcoming bureaucratic consciousness and advocates a better world to come.

Our Hierarchical Roots

Children growing up and widening their territory will again and again hit other people's boundaries, but will gradually learn to be respectful and to follow social rules. They will get used to postponing the fulfilment of a desire and practising discipline, i.e. doing something that contradicts their immediate impulses but seems more sensible under paramount criteria. Children will become increasingly able to observe and control their emotions.

Others are different and this must be respected; but everyone will stick to the rules. Confrontation with different types of authority leads to a differentiated view of power and powerlessness. Various social norms are internalised.

Becoming part of a system causes feelings of security and uneasiness alike. Sometimes it is relieving to us when others make the decisions for us and when all we have to do is play along. At other times, however, we cannot stand being compelled to obey. Sometimes we marvel at the efficiency often displayed by large, structured organisations. At other times we feel that the price we pay for not risking to get fired is just too dear.

We develop gestures of subordination and superiority, which we apply automatically without noticing it. Whenever we meet someone, we feed our sensorium for super- and subordination. We fight about power and being in the right, we judge others and try to justify our own views and positions.

Characteristic fears:

- fear of not living up to other people's expectations and failing to please them (I must do what the others want me to, or else I will be despised, exposed, or excluded)

- fear of being overrun or lagging behind new developments (the world is getting more and more complicated; I cannot keep up with the developments; the society is about to fall apart)
- fear of losing control and sight of the developments (the situation is getting out of hand, it makes me feel insecure; I must keep things in order)
- fear of making mistakes or being blamed for doing so (if I make mistakes, if I am not good enough, I may lose my position within the hierarchy or my place within the society).
- fear of losing face (if I don't behave well, I may be despised, shamed, or belittled)

Negative Fixations:

- aspiration for and sustenance of power for power's sake (the dictator)
- abuse of power for oppressing other people (the tyrant)
- struggle against all forms of power (the rebel without a cause)
- support of law and order without asking what it is for (the servile)
- feelings of shame for deviating from norms or failing to meet expectations (the ashamed)
- permittance of injustice for fear of punishment (the cowardly)

Resources:

- understanding for rules and organising principles
- sensitivity for social differences and manners
- detecting other people's needs and expectations
- foregoing the immediate fulfilment of desires
- sense of fairness and justice
- loyalty and reliability
- sense of duty and team spirit

Exercises

Reflections on Patterns of Authority

purpose: getting a clear understanding of authority and learning to apply it

indications: problems with superiors a with exerting authority

Instructions: What, in your opinion, makes for good authority: what qualities should authorities have, what qualities should they not have? What do you need from a person giving you instructions so you can follow them without resistance?

If you yourself are in a powerful position where you give instructions: when are you satisfied with yourself, when do you blame yourself? How can you tell if those you give instructions to, follow them with or without inner resistance? What do you learn about yourself when noticing that someone is following your instructions grudgingly, openly refuses to comply, or is thwarting your plans?

This exercise may help clarify your own view of authority, how you want to be treated by authorities, and how you can use your social power in a good way.

Familiarisation with and Dissolution of One's Shame

purpose: becoming aware of one's triggers for sense of shame

indications: lack of self-confidence and assertiveness due to internalised shame

Instructions: Examine your sense of shame. It draws your attention to the fact that you have broken a social rule or that you think you have. When was the last time you felt ashamed or embarrassed? Which rule was concerned? How did other people react? Did you hurt or irritate anyone? In that situation, what was the fear behind your sense of shame?

Make it clear to yourself that in your own view you did the best you could in that situation. Maybe you were just not aware that you annoyed or hurt somebody. Maybe you still owe someone an explanation or an apology. Forgive yourself as well and then bury the past of this situation: imagine walking out of the situation: turn around, look towards the future and walk into it. Walk into that direction until you have reached a point where you can turn around to the old situation without getting unpleasant feelings.

This exercise can help sharpen your awareness of your own inner sense of shame and aid you in handling it. It can help you to get over embarrassing situations.

Finding Security Within

purpose: building up an inner sense of security independent of the environment

indications: fear of loss in one's private and professional life, irritability to outer influences

Instructions: Take a few deep breaths and relax. Get in contact with your inner self. Think of situations in your life that frighten you, major and minor ones. Picture these fears as waves on a lake and allow yourself to sink deep down into that lake, deeper and deeper until you find a place of peace and rest at the bottom of the lake. Far away from this place, the waves of worry and of fear roll about, while you rest deep down within your own self.

If you pay regular visits to this place of peace and serenity within, you will find yourself increasingly at ease in everyday life. Nothing will bring you out of balance, because you will know that your security lies within your own self and that's where you can find it.

* * *

These exercises concerning hierarchical consciousness can help you gain a deeper understanding of your own patterns of behaviour towards authorities, which correspond to your personal socialisation.

It will be easier for you to decide which of these patterns are helpful and which are inhibiting. You will find out in what way social structures can make you feel safe and what responsibilities and burdens they can relieve you of. You may also realise that your inner well-being and feeling of security do not depend on external institutions but are rooted deep within you.

Stage 4: Materialistic Consciousness – Man and Achievement

Key aspects:
domination of nature, economic individualism, competition, consumption, success, fear of individual decline

With a grin of satisfaction on his face, Jacob closed the books. Business was going well. There were some debtors who worried him, but the properties and factories impounded by him were pouring money into his cash box. And there were fantastic new sources of income opening up for him. He had long had the idea of equipping a few ships, which were to sail the new waterways and return with great profits. The risk was considerable, yet if one out of two ships returned the investment would be more than worthwhile. This week he would have a guest from the port and would carefully consider the proposition.

Why should he not take time by the forelock? There were so many great opportunities he could seize. The days when interest rates were viewed with mistrust and suspicion were over. The powerful needed money and they were grateful to those who could lend it to them. Wasn't he in fact the one in power? He did not need all that splendour and vain self-representation the aristocrats had to rely on. He preferred to remain in the background, and his safety was based on numbers and figures carefully recorded in books.

****

The offer was enticing; certainly there'd be more work involved, but the promised salary was in fact 30 per cent higher than what he had got so far. The house in the country could then be financed; and a second car for Melissa, which had long been a subject of debate, would no longer be a problem either. How surprised she would be the day he handed her the car key, along with a lush bunch of roses!

Konrad was wondering if he should talk to her about his new position. He would have to say that the change was inevitable, that he would? He would have to prepare her for his having to spend more time in the firm and having to go on a business trip every once in a while. After all, the advantages were quite convincing: the days of financial troubles would be over. They could draw on plentiful resources – long-distance travels, new furniture, better schools for the children!

Sure, the children adored him; they really needed him around. He would simply have to save the weekends for the children. The boss had said that even the weekends would sometimes be crammed with in-house trainings and meetings, but once or twice a year could not hurt, or could it?

Another enticing aspect was that he could finally put some more of his ideas into effect: in his new position he would have people under him that he could delegate some of his routine work to. As head of department he could be really proud of himself, and if he put his shoulder to the wheel, yet other steps on the career ladder would be possible.

A New Dynamic

To some, the hallmark of the breakthrough of materialistic consciousness was the Cartesian shift. René Descartes (1596-1650) saw the world as split into two categories – material and spiritual –, which he thought of as unconnected. The world of material objects is inanimate, and souls are immaterial.

In this, Descartes had of course been influenced by many of the earlier philosophers (the basic assumptions of materialistic thinking had already been formulated in Greek antiquity by Leucippus and Democritus). By the beginning of the modern era, however, European societies had changed in such a way and to such an extent as to allow materialism to become more than just a caprice of mainstream philosophy. Materialism would form the basic pattern of a whole new consciousness, which continues to affect the lives of people today.

Some of the early proponents of materialistic consciousness adopt the biblical command, „Subdue the earth“, for their motto. The motive of power, which urged the heroes of individualism to flee the confines of tribal tradition, was harnessed and channeled with varied success by the hierarchical system. Now it finds a new victim, one that bureaucratic consciousness has already begun to bring under control: nature. Man's lust for power is now unreservedly unleashed on nature – including human nature, i.e. the human body. The body is treated like a machine, while the mind turns into a haughty designer of a human society to which is promised a life without hardship (the alleged purpose of capitalism). Nature and the human body are deprived of all things necessary for man to "forever" overcome his fear of doom.

Materialistic ideas create a powerful political dynamic, which challenges the established hierarchical systems and brings them down in bloody revolutions (especially in France). This dynamic challenges the rigid absolutist concept of power and is capable of triumphing over it literally overnight (as it did on August 5th/6th, 1789). At the onslaught of the revolutionaries, the *ancien régime* collapsed like a house of cards. The values of liberty, equality and fraternity proved to be the undoing of the established absolutist hierarchy. According to the materialistic view of the world, there are no divine privileges determined by birth. Rights are determined by the people, and do not obey the laws of nature like physical objects. All that is not subject to the laws of nature and can therefore be controlled by man must be organised by the human race on the basis of agreement. This is the democratic principle of materialism.

The Power of Numbers and Figures

The principle of measurability and the consequent predominance of figures utterly deprive tradition of its power. Another constitutive element of the tribal community thus disappears from view. Every rule is determined by man; tradition no longer counts as an argument: the concept of tradition is now regarded as arbitrary and "subjective", clashing with the viewpoint of the proponents of measurability.

People then begin to count and measure whatever they can. Houses, inhabitants, fields, and forests – nothing escapes the eagle eyes of the servants of measurability. Eventually, every square inch can unambiguously be allocated to a proprietor, who is identifiable by his number.

The principle of equality is only formally accepted by the materialists. It results from the leading principle of numbers and not from a qualitative appreciation of human dignity. Just as every number differs from another in an abstract sense (1 differs from 2, because 1 is not or cannot be 2) but does belong to the same category (both 1 and 2 are part of the same numerical sequence), in the same way people are seen as essentially the same by materialistic consciousness.

The digital age has begun: the age of efficiency, speediness, and superficiality: the age of the levelling of qualities. Digitalisation, which began with the introduction of written language at the stage of hierarchical consciousness, has since been conquering area after area in the social and cultural spheres.

On the basis of the abovementioned abstract inequality of numbers, a novel ideological radicalness comes into being. Numbers are indisputably and irrefutably different from one another. 1 is not and will never be 2. This mathematical principle is now applied to social and political areas of life, where it signifies: either you are with me or against me, *tertium non datur*. A culture of transitions and nuances succumbs to the power of absolute differentiation, based on the tyranny of numbers and figures.

Ferdinand de Saussure suggested the differentiation between analogous and digital representation, which can help us understand how materialism works. There are two fundamentally different modes of relation between the sign and the signified. Their relation is of an analogous nature if there is a similarity between them, i.e. if the signified is imitated with regard to form by the sign. Thus, the nature of the signified is recognised. The digital mode of representation came with the introduction of written language, where the relation between the signified (i.e. reality) and the sign (i.e. the representation of reality) is arbitrary. While pictographic systems of writing are more of a borderline case, syllabic and alphabetic scripts clearly develop further and further away from reality. Hence, the written word "leaf" no longer bears any similarity to what it denotes.

The great advantage of digitalisation is that it is universally applicable. Digital systems of representation cannot be decoded by intuition but must first be mastered, yet once they have they can be used in many different ways. For instance, it takes only just above two dozen abstract signs to record all the works of world literature. Even abstract subject matter is easier to represent digitally. Digitalisation is thus a precondition for the evolution of science.

In materialism, the digital mode of representation is given greater status than the analogous mode. Descartes, for instance, came up with a method by which all objects in existence could be represented by numerical ratios. As the idea of calculation grows in popularity, nature is more and more experienced in an abstract sense, and people undertake to "measure the world". Art becomes a place of refuge for the analogous mode, which is, however, subverted by the development of digital media of representation in the 20th century. Walter Benjamin, for instance, described the loss of the aura of pictures during their reproduction.

What is left of the original message once it has been translated from the analogous into the digital and then again into the analogous mode, which happens whenever music is recorded? How would our perception and cognition change, if one day our mind were to be fed with nothing but digital data? Would we lose our ability to comprehend analogous signals? Our thirst for analogous kinds of experience remains unquenched, which partly explains the commercial success of storytellers such as J.R.R. Tolkien or Michael Ende.

On the other hand, the idea of the digital mode of representation as state of the art still grows in popularity. With the victory march of scientific thought, which became influential in the wake of a thriving materialistic consciousness, an idea of reality becomes prevalent that scarcely demands for any analogous element, except perhaps didactics (for the purpose of passing on knowledge of the digital).

Paradoxically, however, it is scientific thought that ends up curtailing the dominance of materialism. Critical thinking as a basis opens the door for a plurality of world views and approaches, bridging the gap between materialistic and systemic consciousness. Thereby, a one-dimensional idea of reality is transformed into a constructivist one: theories are models of reality, depending on the respective viewpoint and having no objective, absolute ground line.

Thus, the scientific approach of the modern era also provides a basis for the idea of tolerance, which is celebrated in personalistic consciousness: every individual has the right to be the way he or she is and deserves to be respected that way.

Man's triumphant successes in taming nature and raising the efficiency of commercial production are taken for indicators that the adopted logic of figures leads into the right direction. Thus, they open the door for the victory march of materialism. The successes of the new technology based on mathematics are taken as proof for the superiority of this way of thinking. Modern prosperity has enabled a great number of people in the West to lead lives of great convenience. These achievements, however, always come with the one-sided and radical attitude of materialistic mentality.

Bureaucratic consciousness, ostensibly overcome by materialism, regains power under the mathematical rule. A complex modern society is controlled with materialistic efficiency by its bureaucrats, who now employ digital systems. Rulership and exertion of power become abstract, as they are no longer tied to specific people or inter-human relations. The people in power become interchangeable, and the instruments of power outlive the governments using them. In a technocracy, the methods of control once devised by hierarchical consciousness and the principles of quantification come together. Infringement of the law is measured and punished according to the degree of deviation.

There will then be conflicts as well as forms of cooperation between the materialistic system of economy (whose underlying mentality gains more and more power over the society) on the one hand and the administration on the other hand. The power struggle between these two forms of consciousness has not yet ended in a decisive victory for materialism: each time capitalism is in a crisis (which happens more often than its protagonists will care to admit), the old hierarchical systems will regenerate.

Traditional values are replaced by the idea of progress. The future triumphs over the past and becomes the draught horse of the present. Every effort is devoted to it. The idea that everything will get better and better is the materialistic concept of hope. The fact that every external improvement leads to new, unpredictable problems nothing but feeds the mania of zealous effort. When man is swept along by the idea of endless mathematical sequences, there is to him no limit to progress and no time to rest along the way.

Materialism adds to the linear, one-dimensional idea of time (the brainchild of agricultural society) other, parallel strands, which must be considered simultaneously. Industrial production does not have just one but many different dimensions of time: apart from production there are certain other aspects such as the sales (marketing), which are considered at the same time. This leads to the creation of time loops, where strategic thinking anticipates possible sales and is applied to production.

It is thus the multidimensional market that sets more than one time horizon. Thus, to fully comprehend the complexity of materialistic society, many simultaneous processes must be thought of as the constituents of a whole.

For the individual, this parallel connection is chronically overwhelming. Latent nervousness, as characteristic for materialistic consciousness, spreads far and wide: the anxiety over never being on time and never getting time to relax.

Materialistic consciousness grows most dynamic and powerful in the intent of improving – or even perfecting – human living conditions. This progress in the right direction is to be made by producing improved articles. This optimism can make available great creative resources. It leads millions of people out of a life of privation. Everything is changeable, nothing has to stay the same, and we can share our ideas for the future and realise them. The idea that life is full of opportunities instils feelings of freedom and boundlessness. Indeed, to the children of materialistic consciousness, "the sky is the limit". It is this impetus that encouraged man to radically change the face of the Earth over just a few hundred years and exploit it for the purpose of greater comfort.

However, the inevitable damage caused by the urge to reorganise and reshape for ever greater freedom cannot be fixed by the means and patterns of thought of this stage. And the inner price the individual has to pay for his restless way of living, namely his loss of emotional qualities, can only insufficiently be compensated for at this stage.

The Principle of Permanent Change

At the materialistic stage, nothing is permanent. The products of the economy, the main focus of this stage, never last forever. Tradition in materialism is not better off: fashions change faster than the seasons, and people constantly change their addresses or at least their inner lives. Inter-human relations become more fleeting and detached. The new mobility leads to greater geographical fluctuation, and the increased velocity the technological inventions of the modern era has made possible removes man not only from his birthplace but from nature in general, in which so great a speed is unknown.

The message is: nothing lasts, and you may not rest, or else the "fury of disappearance" (as Hegel puts it) will devour you. Constant change is the blessing and the curse of capitalism, whose protagonists toil away as if they wanted to prove to themselves over and over again that they are damned. They suffer from the terrible situation they themselves cause through their actions, thinking, "that's just the way it is, there is no alternative". The nature of things, the nature of the social order ostensibly leaves us no other option but to exploit ourselves and to attempt escaping the undertow of natural change by the means of a permanent, factitious destruction and renewal.

Long before modern materialism, Buddha himself taught that all things must pass. This insight is an important aspect of holistic consciousness, and materialistic consciousness inadvertently and unknowingly paves the way for it. At this stage, however, the fear of drowning in the flood of change and unpredictability is still prevalent. The only way out, it is thought, is by toiling away, building a dam against the flood of change – which can, however, not be expected to hold out forever. Yet the soul cannot come to rest unless it realises that it does not have to tie itself to anything in the material world to find inner peace.

Man's understanding of reality changes dramatically under the influence of materialism. To most people nowadays the radical Cartesian split is the quintessence of reality. The only way we can gain undisputable knowledge is through a combination of sensory perception and scientific interpretation on a mathematical basis. All else is unreal or real on a primitive level. The earlier mystical concepts of reality are referred to as obsolete and thought of as superstitious.

The reason why the materialistic concept of reality is so successful is that it is easy to communicate it. It suggests itself as the connecting link of a global community that evolved in the age of materialism. It serves as common ground for everyone to agree on. Local narrative traditions, on the other hand, are degraded to pre-realities. The measureable world alone is beyond the sphere of randomness, serving as an iron yardstick for all other products of the human mind. In all the hustle and bustle of materialistic performance, this unquestionable reality serves as a foundation and is therefore defended by all means available.

The fact that every stage of consciousness develops its own concept of reality is ignored at this stage, partly because materialistic consciousness has such a strangely ahistorical quality. Once accepted in the sphere of power, capitalism is thought of as an eternal and all-pervasive structure that overthrows animate and inanimate entities alike and is not subject to historical evanescence.

Capitalism

One cause for the emergence of the new system of economy is the rising demand for finances to support the powers that be. Initially, it was no more than a marginal aspect of the hierarchical systems of the European middle-ages. Many members of the middle classes that were independent of the feudal system served aristocratic households as "managers of finances" and thus represented a new idea of economy, which would eventually cast a spell over the entire world. They realised that if they played their cards right they might one day be as powerful as the aristocracy themselves, or even surpass them in power. Emancipatory valour, which caused the emergence of the class of aristocracy, is transferred from the cities of the Late Middle Ages to the profane sphere of production and trade.

The big wars of the modern era involved efforts to defend different systems of hierarchy against others. They resulted from the tendency of such systems to build up and sustain power. However, it does not take a war for capitalism to flourish; on the contrary, war may seriously destabilise the economy and lead to regression to pre-capitalistic forms of economy.

Capitalism, however, does not have the means to call a halt to war or prevent it from breaking out: it has borrowed the principle of competition from hierarchical consciousness and has generalised it.

In capitalism, all the safety the bureaucratic system can offer is lifted. The bureaucratic system granted people who conformed to its standards a livelihood by the simplest of means and reserved all luxury for the fortunate few. Yet it still conveyed the feeling that affiliation, the basic principle of community and a central aspect of tribal life, was guaranteed.

Industrialisation replaces the natural membership of "well-behaved" subjects with the principle of performance. Whoever works efficiently enough belongs to the community; whoever does not is an outcast. Performance is the ticket to materialistic society. He who works gets a chance. According to the Soviet constitution of 1936: "He who does not work, neither shall he eat."

Fear for survival is thus incorporated in all areas of human life. Stress becomes an aspect of the perceived normal living conditions, to which the body must adapt, no matter what. Walking through a shopping mall in a Western city, one will find it nearly impossible not to be affected by the prevalent atmosphere of nervousness and tension.

Even the norms for performance are focussed at infinity. The actual performance is never good enough. In the hierarchical system already there were attempts at quantifying performance. However, as the chief aim was to sustain power, there was no need to raise the standards for performance. In industrial capitalism, on the other hand, these are ever blown up by the terrible machinations of Competition, the daughter of the market-god. Capitalism is a dog-eat-dog world: if you are better than your rival, you outbid him until he has "had it". Then the tail-lights of the next rival appear on the horizon; he must be overtaken as well, so you have to work even harder.

Only the body can set limits to the blowing up of performance norms. But people are exchangeable: if one body fails, it is simply replaced by another. That is the logic of meritocracy, which in itself is utterly ruinous. It would have collapsed long ago if there were no supporting institutions or legally introduced buffer zones. Part of the old hierarchical structure had to be kept so that capitalism would not destroy itself and everything around it. Personalistic elements, too, contribute to the softening of the brutal basic structure of the system. Still, most people in the industrial world have internalised this logic and feel motivated by it.

With every upward movement of the spiral of achievement of the material world, man is further removed from nature. People start to surround themselves with synthetic material on the outside, and little by little their inner world likewise turns into synthetic material, which is due to the industrialisation of entertainment.

Those who have not made it are despised. Therefore, the people of a meritocracy tend to patronise and debase foreign cultures that have not yet surrendered their will to the principle of performance. The colonial powers considered themselves superior to the pre-industrial peoples, whom they overthrew, exploited, and declared inferior. But the impoverished people at the periphery of affluent societies, too, are regarded with a haughtiness implicit in statements such as, "Everyone who wants to can make it". Just because a few have made it from rags to riches, it is suggested that everyone can.

The Attitude towards Reproduction in Materialism

One aspect of human life where self-deconstruction is in particular effect is that of reproduction. To meritocratic society, children get in the way of performance, minimising one's chances of getting a job and not contributing to the insurance of survival – on the contrary, they represent a burden. Men and women alike submit to the expectations of society. The tribal motives of getting children so that life may continue and the tradition may survive, are considerably weakened. Even prospective grandparents are wary of motivating their children to start a family: they know how hard it is to raise children in a capitalist society.

Contraception and abortion are meant to "safeguard" people against "surprises". If there is, however, going to be a birth, it is planned so as to reduce the probability of complications. The form of delivery characteristic for meritocracy is the planned Caesarean section, free of pain for the mother and according to schedule. The need of the child to be delivered in a healthy manner is ignored. The baby is required to perform: an early load of meritocratic burdens. When the mother goes into labour, individual performance is lauded as the most important aspect, the best guarantor against pain; nature is to interfere with it as little as possible. It is at times like these that the estrangement from nature and the maxim of performance are passed on to the next generation.

Materialistic consciousness thus has the baleful urge to create the greatest possible distance to nature; and often it manages to do so by entering the organic plane and there affecting a change that poses a threat to life itself.

The predominance of the intellect in society goes hand in glove with another form of degradation of women: for quite some time, they are almost completely removed from the exciting world of business and thought. Male intellectual heroes of materialism believe that they have the monopoly on the new form of consciousness, ascribing to themselves the most important qualification: logical, sensible thinking. Schopenhauer's interpretation to that effect is just one among many examples for this attitude. Women are said to lack intellectual talent and instead to possess an excess of emotions. As emotions are associated with the body, they are debased along with it and regarded as inferior to thought for their uncontrollable, incalculable and unpredictable nature. All the phenomena that materialistic consciousness cannot express mathematically are declared worth- and meaningless. Therefore, in the 19th century scientific psychology first began to try measuring feelings – which task it has never convincingly accomplished to this day.

In materialistic consciousness, the dichotomy of nature and the mind is taken to extremes. This form of consciousness could not move away any further than this from its own foundation. This is also why at this stage patriarchalism, i.e. the systematic debasement of women, comes up against an impenetrable boundary.

Socialism

As an answer to capitalism with its endeavours to unleash the monster of unbridled, reckless individual greed onto the world, socialism evolves. Socialism uses the consternation of personalistic consciousness: people may not exploit other people. People may not quantitatively assess other people. The norms for performance must not be inhumane. The economy should serve the people, not vice-versa.

Socialists try to apply a personalistic concept of community in order to curtail or even overcome the exploitative circumstances of capitalism. However, they fail because they underestimate the difficulty of planning a national economy. In trying to control and put their ideals before the market, the god of capitalism, they are bound to fail.

At the systemic stage of consciousness, it becomes plain that a part of the system cannot control the system: every attempt to this effect will cause a new system that is beyond control.

Moreover, socialism is in many ways tied to materialistic consciousness. While its pathos and moral authority stem from personalistic consciousness, which defines its progressive and revolutionary impetus, behind this facade, certain alliances with the undercurrents of materialism must be noted, which do not fit in with the personalistic message. Socialism does not rely on the evolutionary development of consciousness (Feuerbach already departs from Hegel here) but on the development of technology, which capitalism initiated.

Technology is to triumph over the world and help mankind to an abundance of goods, which need only be distributed fairly amongst the people for paradise to become reality. But as Pier Paolo Pasolini pointed out, as soon as human conscience sells out to the production of goods, it, too, is treated like an object. The laws of a production organised by scientific principles seem to have more power over society than the ideals of enlightened reason.

Socialism suffers from its own anti-religion stance, which it borrowed from materialistic thinking. Its religion is materialism, and its delusion is that social processes are controllable. As at all stages previous, what becomes apparent here is that every form of consciousness, as long as it has not reached the plane of holistic awareness, develops a form of religiosity and projects onto the divine the basic motivations inherent in the respective stage.

In socialism, the idea of utter sovereignty over nature, which made possible the Industrial Revolution and the breakthrough of capitalism, is appropriated and applied to rearranging the social order. Materialism fails when nature gets out of hand and deprives its would-be master of his basis for life: the body of the materialist becomes the victim of his own lust for power. Socialists mean to prevent all evils by extensive planning, which involves the calculation of the needs of the body. Thus, exploitation happens on an even deeper level, where the illuminating rays of conscious insight cannot reach: and thus, individual development is inhibited.

These ties of socialism to capitalism and materialism caused the Soviet Union and other socialist systems to betray their own humanitarian ideals and fall back on the cruel, heavy-handed ways of the hierarchical stage: they led to the introduction of inhuman and fiercely repressive dictatorship.

The boom of atheist models, however, is not restricted to the sphere of socialism. The god of capitalism is the market, whose uncounted minions worship the ground he treads, needing no other god. The invisible hand that matches supply and demand, the unfathomable texture of actions and reactions, which can form new constellations in the blink of an eye: these secret forces of capitalism suffice to fulfil the capitalist's need for mysticism. His boundless greed must protect itself against feelings of guilt and moral responsibility. Atheism provides this kind of protection. The guilty conscience that hierarchical consciousness implanted into the minds of the people turns into cynicism in materialism. The materialist is allowed to riot to the full in his greedy obsessions, provided he is successful; and if the winds of market forces do turn against him, he is to simply sail in another direction. He regards acquisition as an end in itself for which no justification is necessary.

Self-reproduction in Addiction

Materialism directs people's main focus to material objects and has the aim of quantifying their value: and thus it creates a mechanism of obsession that is second to none. If people define their personal value over material objects, they are caught in a tenacious web of endless wishes and desires. Then, every fulfilment of a wish creates in the individual the wish for more of the same or the next best thing. Nothing in the material world can fulfil a yearning, because yearnings are really for deeper forms of satisfaction. All that material objects can provide is the short-lived illusion that we have reached the goal of our quest. As soon as the fascination for a newly acquired material object starts to die down, there is a new goal promising happiness.

Drug addiction becomes a major problem in the materialistic society and mirrors it. The drug addict isolates the morbid pattern that drives the society on and in destroying himself takes it to utter extremes. His addiction indicates a desperate search for the love he never had but also a longing to break free from the shackles of a cruel, inhumane social system.

The decent citizens of meritocracy are appalled and disgusted, and they sit down to watch the latest crime series, eat the most extravagant brand of potato chips and sip the latest soft drink, as if they had nothing in common with the drug addict. The average consumer of material goods is not dependent on one particular substance or pattern of behaviour like the junkie but on the multitude of possible stimuli. He will, for instance, take one holiday trip after the other, without suspecting that he might have some kind of addiction. However, if for some reason he cannot go on his long-anticipated vacations, he will miss not only the recreation but also a scrap of self-affirmation, social prestige, and happiness.

Admittedly, the materialistic average addict can replace one thing that is currently unavailable or that he will never get with another; he is not fixated on a certain substance like the addict to heroin but the object of his desire is flexible and variable. If, however, he does not consume anything new for a while, he will be nervous and restless, until he finally gets hold of something new.

What mobilises these mechanisms of obsession, obvious or rather more subtle, is the fear of lack, i.e. the fear of dying when there is nothing left to sustain life. What keeps people alive from the beginning is primarily love from other people (for as babies we do know that if we are loved, all other things we need for survival will be provided for as well). Thus, wherever lack of affection has become the driving force of development, some form of compensation is necessary, which the system of materialism excessively provides. Substitutes for love are permanently invented, produced, and thrown on the market.

We flee from the moment when nothing new is happening, when no material object we find can attract our attention, and when no yearning is strong enough to excite our curiosity. Emptiness, devoidness of material objects makes us feel our lack of affection and the pain connected with it. The materialistic system of production with its endless light entertainment programme makes it possible for us not to clearly feel this pain. That is why we never want to part with the system. It seems the best system imaginable.

We all know how it works. First there was only the cinema, and people were perfectly happy with watching a new film every week. Then television came. People were content with one or two programmes every day. Then the television programme was expanded and there was entertainment around the clock. Then cable and satellite television were introduced. Thus, the web of entertainment becomes denser and denser. No moment should be spare, and at no point in time should there be just one option: every moment should offer a great number of attractive alternatives. That is the freedom we ask for: the freedom of choosing the way in which we want to be stimulated and distracted.

The machinery of entertainment represents the immaterial form of the addictive society or its essence. It programs our mind to sequences of fleeting stimuli and constant change. Entertainment serves to suppress fear. This is why we quickly get bored with watching a tree that does not move. Even nature is interesting only in that it offers new phenomena: a new waterfall, a zoological or botanical species we have never seen before – and finally, a natural disaster of unprecedented magnitude, which satisfies the hunger for all things vast and terrible.

Man's horrified enjoyment of the raging natural forces mirrors his increasing tendency towards instrumentalising his relationship with the environment. His distanced relationship to nature enables him not only to unscrupulously exploit natural resources but to adopt a more impartial attitude towards violence in general. While the individual who is the subject of meritocracy is forced to control his own aggressions, the society at large builds up a terrible aggression potential, which is vented in the worst wars ever known to man. But maybe this had to happen for alienated man to have a sobering self-realisation and be forced to take a step onto the succeeding stages of consciousness.

Along the path of the evolution of consciousness, materialism is a bottleneck, a confusing house of mirrors. To the materialist, the world of material objects promises boundless happiness. The digital mode it is used to adopting suggests that there are no limits, and so human desire stretches out to infinity and every temporary fulfilment is followed with the burgeoning of another desire. Since materialism takes the greatest possible distance to nature – you cannot go any further than that –, it is also capable of posing the greatest possible threat to the very basis for human life.

Whether mankind will be able to rise to this challenge is as yet uncertain. So far only a small minority of the world population has fully entered this phase. But this small minority has so greatly damaged the biosphere that it remains unclear whether things will ever return to the way they were. Who knows what will happen when the rest of the world lives the dream of materialism, indulging in cars, refrigerators, air conditioners, and enormous quantities of meat?

We can only hope that, once they have acquired their own wealth, the regions of the world that have up to now been affected negatively rather than positively by materialistic culture will be more alert to its dangers and try to avoid the mistakes that have been made in the past.

It took European civilisation about 500 years to fully develop capitalism. The U.S.A. already made it within 200 years. And the tigers of East Asia were a lot faster still. Therefore, we may hope that more and more countries will make the leap to affluent societies within a shorter period of time. It is impossible, however, to predict whether they will walk the path beyond, the path of self-limitation, at a faster pace than the absolutely hesitant Western societies have shown so far.

It is not yet decided, then, if the bottleneck of history leads to a dead end, so that the succeeding stages of consciousness cannot be realised on a broader basis, or if it is really a birth canal, which in a fight between life and death finally brings new life. At the personalistic stage, man's alienation from himself by capitalism becomes clear: the soul is lost in the blizzard of the economy. Abandoning the capitalist view of the world and entering into personalistic consciousness increases in popularity. Thus, capitalism is no longer taken for granted and loses its dynamic quality. This development is, however, still in its initial stages, as there are many places around the world that are still in the process of adopting the system of capitalism. Still, there is a certain global trend of replacing quantitative principles with qualitative ones, and the demand for quality, inter alia quality of life, has begun to pose a serious threat to the absolutist regency of capitalism.

At the systemic stage, the functioning of capitalism is generalised. The market becomes one among many systems and can no longer assert its dominance over the others. The political, ecological, social, developmental, and cultural spheres are granted equal status in the overall context of society, and there is a strong connection between the market and other areas. Here's an example: the success of the economy becomes dependent on values from other areas. The ecological commitment of a firm, for instance, turns into an indispensable and profitable image-enhancing factor.

At the universalistic stage, finally, the established mechanisms of capitalism serve to balance the production of goods and optimise distribution. The locations with the best production possibilities are determined according to principles of the market. On the quantitative level, equipartition among the community is ensured. As the basic motivations of the materialistic stage (greed and fear for survival) have been disempowered, it is possible for the market to function as a systemic medium of balance.

It is only by overcoming individual unscrupulousness, not by taking it to extremes ("private vices, public benefits" according to Bernard Mandeville), that the market can be shown to advantage. Problematically, capitalism takes advantage of people's greed and fear to recruit them and encourages these two motivators in everyone. If one is just as greedy and anxious as the other, the system of greed is bound to collapse. Therefore, in order to survive, capitalism must embrace certain social and political values, which, if put into practice, might eventually lead to a higher stage of organisation – the systemic stage.

Our Attachment to the Stage of Materialism

Little children live in a world where imagination and sensory perception are connected and intermingled. The understanding of reality adults (of Western society) entertain takes a long time to develop in a child. As this understanding evolves at the threshold to school age, the infant learns about the concept of performance and how it differs from that of play – in that one makes an effort to achieve something that is not imminently connected with the satisfaction of a need but in the long run promises profit. The child learns to shelve imminent organic needs. Praise, on the other hand, becomes more important to it. The infant needs confirmation in what it has achieved so far so that it will feel motivated to achieve more.

At the threshold to school age, we start to explore our possibilities of and limitations to our performance and compare ourselves to others. We become more aware of the mechanisms of competition and will feel the conflict between solidarity with our peers and individual triumph. We get to know "objective" ways of assessment and are "measured". The school system takes us under its wings and prepares us for "life". We are told that the serious part of life has begun. We start to feel a lot of pressure and forget how to relax.

How can we find out in what way materialistic consciousness influences us as individuals? Reflecting on the temptations of this stage and leaving them behind could be our biggest step towards inner liberation. For as we have seen, materialistic consciousness represents the biggest challenge for inner growth. Let us, therefore, name the fears, fixations and resources from this stage in our history.

Characteristic Fears:

- fear of failing
- fear of impoverishment
- fear of losing prestige or privileges
- fear of a life of simplitude and humility
- fear of the irrational

Negative Fixations:

- attachment to success, wealth, and material goods, orientation at superficialities (the career-obsessed profiteer)
- self-sacrification for material ends (the self-exploiter)
- disregard for nature, the body and its needs
- disdain for human relations (the lone wolf)
- contempt for weakness, incompetence, refusal of performance, lack of success (the arrogant performer)

Resources:

- economical and rational thinking
- single-mindedness and willpower
- commitment

Exercises

The habit of clinging to material objects is one of the main causes for hidden fears and neurotic patterns characteristic of the materialistic stage. The more material wealth we own, the more frightened we become of losing it.

Materialistic Fear

purpose: insight into the relativity and evanescence of material objects

indications: agonizing worries about money, possessions and success in life; overestimation of material goods

Instructions: Many of the things that worry us concern the material world: are we earning enough money to lead a life "worth living"? Is our financial situation stable enough to ensure that in a few years' time we will still have enough money?

Breathe in deep and breathe out long, and as you do become aware of your body. Now imagine that your life is soon to end: your body is preparing to die. Realise that at this moment all material objects and material values seem unimportant. There is nothing you can take with you when you leave this world. Imagine that all your worries about material things become groundless. What you really value at this moment is the love you gave and the love you received in life.

Breathe in deep and breathe out long. Become aware of the love you have given and received in life. Without the love of your parents or carers you would not have survived. You got enough love to survive, although you might have wished for more.

Breathe in and breathe out. Ask yourself if there are people in your life you would like to give more love to. If there are, then what is to stop you? Use the time that you have been given on this planet!

This exercise is to help you concentrate on the essential things in life.

Patterns of Stress

purpose: witnessing strain and stress in everyday life, detecting little stressors, recognising tendencies that may lead to chronification of stress

indications: nervousness, high irritability, sleeping disorders, various psychosomatic complaints

Instructions: Journal of stress: Every night, set aside a little time to take notes on the following subject: what was it that caused pressure today? Were you stressed when driving a car, when crossing a street, when waiting in a queue at the supermarket, when walking in a crush on the pavement, when reading an upsetting headline in a daily newspaper, or when arguing with a colleague at work? Write down the causes for stress, no matter how important or unimportant they may seem to you.

If you regularly make entries you may gain a greater awareness of when you relax in everyday life. Now every time you feel pressure, make sure of relaxing. Let your breath be your helpmate: breathe deep and in a relaxed manner, or make use of another relaxation technique you have learned.

An exercise for motorists: sitting in a car in a traffic jam is the perfect situation for dissolving fear. What happens in a traffic jam is that we want to go on, even desparately in most cases because we are missing an important appointment, but we are stuck. Consequently, we will feel afraid, frustrated, and aggressive; but that will not change anything about the situation. As soon as you notice that you are suffering under the situation, watch your breath. Your breath can take you back to the present moment; it can take your focus from the external situation to your inside, to your own self. You realise that you are just there, that the external situation is the way it is, that there is nothing you can do about it. You become confident that you will master the challenges that may ensue from the time lag, as there are so many other things that you have mastered in your life. You use the opportunity to pacify your mind and summon inner strength. And probably you can barely wait for the next traffic jam, another opportunity for doing this exercise!

If you look into your stress behaviour, you can contribute greatly to the improvement of your own health and quality of life. Overlooked pressure can increase one's basic tension and may be the cause for exhaustion and illness.

Resolution of Stress

purpose: being able to diagnose chronic stress in oneself, so that precautions might be taken to prevent the impairing effects this might have on one's health

indications: stress and stress-related illnesses

Instructions: Chronic stress is the most characteristic illness of the materialistic stage. If you want to know whether you are currently under stress, just watch your breath: your breath rate at rest should be between 10 and 15 breaths per minute. If you breathe faster, you may be suffering from chronic stress. Even when you are not feeling stressed, your body will act as if you were in a threatening situation.

You should exhale in a relaxed manner. Can you just let go of the breath flowing out, without pressure, without trying to control, like a hand that you just let fall? Is your exhalation effortless, like a feather that is floating to the ground on its own, or do you have to make an effort to let the air escape from your lungs? Take your time and keep watching your breath, until you notice that it is becoming easier and easier.

If you suffer from chronic stress, take care to relax more often. Use your spare time to take care of yourself, choose activities that give you pleasure without demanding performance.

* * *

These exercises may help you manage better in the complex world of consumption and entertainment. We must practise again and again to remain autonomous from the excess of stimuli and incentives we are daily confronted with, and to listen for our inner voice to tell us what is good for us, what we really need and how we really want to act.

Moreover, it is almost vitally imperative that we make ourselves familiar with and change our attitude towards stress by cultivating our awareness of the body. What this also ties in with is our relationship to nature, which in the world of materialism we must every now and then uncover anew.

Stage 5: Personalistic Consciousness – Human Self-Realisation

It is personalities, not principles, that move the age.

(Oscar Wilde)

When we have first found ourselves, we must understand how from time to time to lose ourselves and then to find ourselves again. – This is true on the assumption that we are thinkers. A thinker finds it a drawback always to be tied to one person.

(Friedrich Nietzsche, Human, All-Too-Human II, 306)

Key aspects:
uniqueness of the individual, human rights, overcoming of conventions, appreciation of art, cult of genius, fear of loss of self

Clara retired to the arbour. The fully scribbled notebook lay on her lap. It had been an exceedingly interesting afternoon. At last, the Count of K. had followed the invitation she had expressed a long time beforehand. And how delightfully had he spoken of his journey to France – words like the wind of change, bearing new, bold ideas. In this day and age, where most people only ever thought of business or the code of decent manners, such a spirit was priceless. If only more people woke up from their narrow-mindedness and ventured to think for themselves! How very few had realised that a new age was dawning, in which the great values of humanity would at last be shown to advantage.

Enthusiastically, they had talked over coffee and cake. As a parting gift, he had given her a nobly shaped flacon with a new perfume creation straight from Paris – what a wonderful fragrance!

In the evening, there would be a concert: a wonderful Italian-style serenade, a warm, refreshing bath for the soul. It was the only form of art her husband could be enthusiastic for.

***

Konrad was walking along the forest path, immersed in his own heart. He was deeply moved by what he had experienced within: the yearning for being understood, for being loved, and the idea of what might be a better life. He would have to talk about this in quiet with his wife. Of course, he had also realised what it was that he had been doing wrong, and he would have to talk about that, too. He would have to make a complete turn-around or at least change a lot of things in his life. He had sacrificed several years to his career, and now he began to realise what the price was. His heart worried him, his digestion was malfunctioning, and he suffered from sleeping disorders. He had begun to feel alienated from his wife and his children. And when was the last time he felt really happy? When had he laughed with all his heart? When had he been joyful and lighthearted?

What did he really want from life? How did he really benefit from hoarding money, and from the job he was doing, where more and more was demanded while his performance was less and less appreciated.

He felt the fragrant air of the forest and listened to the chirping of the birds. What a soothing quality, what a comfort it was that emanated from the trees, which were softly rocking in the wind! As if everything could still turn out right!

From the Uniformity of the Manifold to Quality

This stage is not announced by dramatic fanfares or visible changes in the landscape. By subtly influencing the intellectual-emotional climate, it insinuates itself into a society dominated by materialism and, slowly but surely, waters it down. It does not instrumentalise governmental institutions or military machines but relies on its own persuasive power, in the name of "humanity".

The old philosophical aphorism "*individuum est ineffabile*" is a good motto for this stage of consciousness. At the transition between stage 4 and stage 5 it can be translated as: man is not calculable. There is no formula for the essence of man. The depth of human individuality is beyond verbal categorisation and scientific interpretation.

At the materialistic stage of consciousness, the basis of production and organisation to cover man's basic material needs was formed. By new methods based on science and advanced technology, all kinds of food could be produced and distributed among the populace, by which famine and epidemics could be checked in many places of the world. This is the great accomplishment of stage four of consciousness. However, through aggressive European colonialism, new problem areas with abject emergency situations were created. In the areas of welfare, on the other hand, the inner lives of people were plundered.

Human consciousness can now develop one step further: for as soon as physical survival need no longer be the focus of mind and body, internal and external capacities become vacant. Consciousness can now turn to other subjects. Thus, personalistic consciousness is born.

For millions of years, people were primarily concerned with making sure there were enough resources to maintain the body and hold society together. By now, enough goods are produced so that all the people on this planet could have a sufficient basis for life, and even further economic growth of humanity without hunger and existential threats could be ensured if only a working mechanism of distribution were proposed and politically asserted.

The materialistic stage left unresolved the problems of the distribution of wealth, of the integration of centres and peripheries, i.e. all the problems that result from the principle of the equality of all people. Due to its fixation at the market and its coincidences, there is no solution it can or will offer. It is personalistic consciousness that can pave the way for a global community of equal chances and create the necessary intellectual foundation for it. For practical implementation, an additional step is necessary, namely the development towards systemic consciousness. Therefore, at this stage of consciousness there are still highly considerable regional differences: there are the centres of lavish abundance and the large marginal territories, which profit only on a small scale from the developments (if they profit at all) and never appear as associates or agents.

The Difference Between Stage Two and Stage Five

At both these stages individuality rather than community life is held essential, and the single person steps out of the group or mass and creates an image for himself. The step from stage one to stage two can be likened to the detachment and departure of an ovum, which in the life of a fertile woman dissociates from the group of cells in the womb and "embarks" on its journey through the Fallopian tube.

The step from stage four to stage five can be compared with a birth. A complete, if immature, individual being sees the light of day and demands to be seen and loved the way it is. As soon as it is born, this little being yearns to develop and flourish, to realise its own individual personality, so as to render a service to the world.

Thus, at this stage of consciousness the focus is no longer on the mere sustenance of life but on the question how this life can be shown to advantage. The fifth stage of consciousness succeeds the fourth, which in many ways secured the material basis of life and exorcised man's fear for survival. On this foundation the individual can develop freely, creatively organising his life according to his own ideas.

The main motive that marks this new stage of consciousness is the criticism of the uniformity of matter. Material objects, as the philosophers of Greek antiquity already noted, can be put down to the littlest particles, which look all rather identical and mundane – nuclei surrounded by electrons (with large quantities of empty space in between). This is a monotonous landscape that only the lover of microscopes is inclined to haunt.

If we look at the colourful variety of products of the materialistic phase, what we see is highly varied only in appearance. Even though modern production of articles and product design makes every effort to "personalise" its products, to endow them with an individual design, even a special aura, all its endeavours will ever come to is shadows and see-through illusions. Whoever spends a greater amount of time in the halls of consumerism, filled with packages shouting for attention like neglected babies, will become aware of the aversion, the dreariness, the desertedness, which is grounded in the lifelessness of all those articles. Nothing lives but everything pretends to live and implies that in order to live ourselves we must get a hold of it. Having bought the articles, however, we soon realise how transient the happiness is that we wanted to attain by the purchase. After all, we have not bought life but dead things.

This example, which the inhabitants of the centres of affluence are daily confronted with, shows the paradox of the materialistic stage of consciousness and the task of personalistic consciousness. The latter despises the rulership of the dead things. It loathes the dependencies that result from the strife for material goods. And it detests the hollow, lifeless structures and procedures of materialistic society.

Personalistic consciousness means trying to find one's own way and make the world richer with an authentic contribution. It means not continuing what ancient traditions or the process logics of the economy proscribe but displaying one's uniqueness and wanting to be appreciated and admired for it.

The word persona signifies mask; people of the post-materialistic era look for the mask that individualises them, that differentiates them from other masks. This accentuation, however, no longer works with quantitative characteristics as in materialism (expensive brands) but with qualitative ones. The dull, monotonous world of figures is replaced with a realm of nuances and shades of grey.

Personalistic consciousness spells out its principle aversion towards capitalism: not only does it produce a superabundance of articles, it even makes people into commodities, by exploiting their capacities and subjugating them to a logic that alienates them from themselves. Man himself becomes uniform and dull like the articles he produces. It is only the cover that is beautiful, the design that is deeply engraved at the level of organic consciousness, like the fast food that stimulates the taste buds of its eaters until they lose their taste for anything else.

Great effort is devoted to creating this world of illusions, of which everybody zealously partakes although no one really believes in it. The external world is blinding, and inner life is uninteresting. Personalistic consciousness sees through this kind of hypocrisy.

Creativity

The machinery of performance people are subjugated to in materialism puts them under stress, and this stress diminishes their creativity. But further economic growth requires creativity. Thus, in the industrial world of stamping, smoking machines, there have to be oases where the mind can freely develop.

Creativity always leads to surplus, bringing forth useful and useless, usable and trivial things. Part of the creative ideas flows back into the production processes and encourages further growth in them, while others serve the evolution of consciousness and are used for the development of succeeding stages.

Inner Worlds

If one is to divorce from the temptations of materialism, one must focus his attention inward. A person develops within, finding in his soul a refined world of feelings and emotions, which can be included in the discourse and form a counterbalance to the rationality of the materialistic sphere. Emotions become socially acceptable again, as we can tell especially from the differentiations expressed in art.

Amongst the philosophical movements, it is existentialism in particular that points out the chance represented by individual life, as well as the responsibility connected with it. Take your life into your own hand and make something of it: find fulfilment in your own sweet way. Self-realisation is only possible if we manage to break pre-set patterns, such as careers envisaged by the economy, hierarchical dependencies that curtail our creativity, megalomaniac heroic deeds that serve only to raise us above others. Nor should the expectations and plans of our parents or family determine our priorities in life.

The appeal for self-realisation is a call for breaking with conventions, whether they be imposed on the outside or on the inside. Human conscience is to be freed from all content drummed into us by traditionalistic institutions, the church or the state, and becomes merely a formal authority that decides whether the plans we make in life really correspond to our will.

The individual itself is the only yardstick for success in life. It is oriented at itself, striving permanently for liberation from predetermining factors and looking for new perspectives of meaning.

The destination of the inner journey is authenticity. People want to be in tune with themselves, with the core of their being. At all the preceding stages, the focus of attention was on external matters: on the tribe (stage one), on the goal of expansion (stage two), on the system of super- and subordination (stage three), or on material objects (stage four). Now, it is turned within.

In personalistic consciousness, the unique, unmistakable quality of each respective personality is at the centre of attention, while descendency and external appearances fade into the background. The egalitarian treatment of subjects, a means of exercising hierarchical power, is overcome. On this heyday of personal realisation, there is a considerable rise of both artistic and scientific production.

Towards the end of the nineteenth century, most physicists agreed that all essential laws had been discovered and the enigmas of the material world had been explained. It may have been in part for the extremely enthusiastic artistic climate at the turn from the nineteenth to the twentieth centuries that the world of physics would eventually come to rest on a wholly new foundation owing to new theories of relativity and findings of quantum mechanics, which continue to challenge materialism.

The discovery of one's personal, inner life, however, is a veritable Odyssey. The negation of all pre-set possibilities of planning one's life is not sufficient in filling the emptiness of meaning. As soon as personalistic consciousness arrives at a concept of meaning, there is doubt and irritation. The authenticity that is supposedly attained, eventually turns out to be a forgery. Finally, we start to wonder if this person, the goal of our quest for authenticity, really exists. And the pendulum between a happy and a desperate life keeps on swinging.

Turning Inside

By turning inside, we are exposed to our own spiritual vulnerability. Having renounced the external authorities with their untenable promises of safety, we begin to think that we are all alone in bearing our fate. All the strengths and weaknesses of the individual come to surface. The price of the acquisition of freedom by rejecting social norms and ascribed roles is that all the failure and disappointment an individual experiences has to be borne entirely by himself. The psyche exposes itself to the astuteness of other people and especially to one's own scrutiny. It is engraved by all the sensitive minds of this time, broken down into all the different nuances of its sentiments. The quest for individual perfection can never be fulfilling. The steep slopes of unrealised plans for life are now the scene of miserable failure; man's ambitions are defeated by his experience of absurdity rather than the overpowering forces of violence or the unpredictabilities of the market.

As Hölderlin once said, "Where there is danger, a rescuing element grows as well". Psychology and psychotherapy emerge as a reaction to the fears of the personalised souls, who shrink from their own abysses. Instructed spiritual journeys into the shadowy and misty places of the soul propose a way out of the hopelessness of self-adulation.

By exposing to view the subtle emotional worlds of the human soul, man's fragility for inner chaos, not just external influences, becomes apparent. The delicate and highly sensitive become the proponents for turning within. And for the first time, inner life demands equality with outward orientation at the social environment.

If necessary, a member of a tribe had to sacrifice himself for his community, and the tough, uncontrollable environmental conditions allowed only the hardiest people to survive and procreate. To the individualistic hero, vulnerability was almost synonymous with death, the end of all ambitions. Huge physical demands were placed on the subjects of hierarchical societies to satisfy the desires of the ruling classes for luxury and power; on the subject's part, showing weakness often meant forfeiting one's life. Capitalism, finally, tore down every form of sensitivity by praying to its merciless god of performance: only the strong and the successful survive, and weak and unsuccessful people do not get a chance (which social attitude was presented as a law of nature by the exponents of social Darwinism).

Affluence gives those an opportunity to develop who are less fit and competitive than the capitalistic system expects them to be. What many artists anticipated in earlier periods of history now becomes a seal of quality: the more sensitive, the more artistic – the more vulnerable, the more interesting.

The discovery of the subtleties of the mind, ostensibly made out of sheer boredom by educated bourgeois ladies removed from the public sphere, becomes the basis of a new ethic. This ethic transfers the worth of a human being from his quantifiable performance onto qualitative features of his person, thus encouraging the idea that all human beings not only have the right to live but may be appreciated just the way they are, independently of the yardsticks of the earlier stages of consciousness. Starting with the patronising and conscending habit of philanthropism, from this basis a movement grew of protecting and promoting the rights of minorities.

In his novel *The Buddenbrocks*, Thomas Mann describes the awakening of sensitivity in the unfeeling world of business, presenting one of the essential themes of bourgeois culture: the life of the artist and the rank of the arts at a time when materialism reigned supreme, when artistic sensitivity was fearfully referred to as degenerative. Robert Musil, on the other hand, could naturally place his *Man Without Qualities* at the centre of a society already restructured by a change of values. After the catastrophe of World War One, the vulnerability of man was a factor of society too all-pervasive and conspicuous to be ignored: one-legged, half-blind or traumatised veterans, impoverished humanists, and embittered members of the proletariat all bore testimony to it. That is exactly why the National Socialists sought to "eradicate" all that was vulnerable and weak.

With the discovery of the inner world and its wealth of nuances, the values that earlier forms of consciousness backed and instilled in the people are challenged. Every virtue has for its companion a less desirable quality: when practicing the virtue of altruism, for instance, we may at some point become complacent. Friedrich Nietzsche was master in deconstructing highly regarded values and deliberately practiced virtues, the Christian vizard of a merciless capitalist economy. Nietzsche's psycho-philosophical hammer left a scene of shattered, desecrated beliefs from all preceding stages of consciousness, which he referred to as nihilism, and an entire generation of adepts from various different political and philosophical backgrounds tried to profit from this clear-cut.

Again, we may allude to the National Socialist distortion to clarify our meaning: It appeared with the pathos of unequivocalness, which created a huge following, not so much because people believed in the obvious message itself but because they felt understood in their desperation of an unreliable world and their desire for clarity regarding values. The only generation that Nietzsche's orgy of devaluation could really be said to have benefitted is that of post-modernism, whose pragmatics of "anything goes" led to the next stage of consciousness.

Nietzsche's statement, "Without music, my life would be a mistake", leads to the reflection on a form of art that has been influencing the course of evolution. It is a form of expression whose meaning cannot be defined in logical terms. It has the power to influence human consciousness on a deep, fundamental level. Especially from the 18th century onwards, the dynamic of its creative development is accelerated. The background for this is of course increasing affluence as a result of early industrialisation as well as the disempowerment of traditional hierarchical systems. The drive, however, for this flourish of musical art is the differentiation of human self-awareness. This dynamic of musical imagination in Europe is rather unique in the world, assigning music an increasingly important part in shaping human consciousness.

Some musicians reject the social hierarchy and create personal opposite poles to it, becoming symbolic figures of resistance against bureaucratic constraints (the artist as anarchist – consider, for instance, Franz Liszt's splendid head of hair) and against materialism (the artist as idealist preferring commercially unprofitable art to a career). Also, for its materially intangible power, music comes to represent a particular challenge to the materialistic world view.

If in hierarchical systems music was thought primarily to serve the entertainment of the ruler and the integration of the subjects, in the days of capitalism it becomes the favourite comfort of unhappy producers and consumers. After all, it offers a basically harmless experience of contrast: the well-tempered flow of sound helps the individual to recover from the cold, squared world of objects and figures. To the alienated and the lonely, it offers rest and liberation from the agonising idea of performance and success.

The social criticism formulated by music, however, is chiefly inaudible at first and affects the soul on a very deep level, where it nurtures its premonitions for a better world – until they come to the surface and are felt as ardent desires. With Beethoven's music, for instance, the eruptive breakthrough of criticism into the conscious is unmistakable.

Romanticism adopts these ideas and greatly encourages the departure of individual genius. It appeals to the emotional faculty, which in the sober world of materialism has direly been neglected. But now, as opposed to the wild days of early individualism, emotions are cultivated and expressed in a civilised manner – in the form of quiet suffering, repressed anger, ethereal yearning, agonising jealousy, and tongue-tied desperation. Characteristically, they are not realised in a demonstrative or aggressive manner. In the public sphere and in children's private upbringing, strict rules of self-control still prevail. Music makes its contribution to the refinement and cultivation of emotions. The cultivation of emotions in art is left to bourgeois circles: artistic freedom grants access to deep emotional layers.

The bourgeoisie introduces a new form of perceiving music: serious, concentrated listening. While in hierarchical contexts music primarily served to entertain bored feasting aristocrats or to uplift and reform plain churchgoers, the bourgeoisie takes a new approach to it. Bourgeois music lovers want to be touched by music to gain insight into new facets of reality.

Accordingly, especially from Viennese classicism onwards, the variety of strategies for musical expression increases, and the composer ingeniously uses them to encourage the listener's emotional resonance. The recipients feel moved and "recognised" by the music. It offers them a warmth and cosiness between cheerfulness and contemplation, comfort in the anonymity and coldness of a market system knocked about in a sea of coincidence.

Then another prototype of personalistic consciousness is welcomed in the musical arena: the genius. Like the hero of the individualistic age, the genius sets himself apart from the rest. However, his evolutionary spectrum is much broader than that of the warlike individualist, as it is not restricted to the categories of physical strength and agility (as well as the readiness for violence) but presents itself in its mastery over the self and includes all aspects of mind and spirit. Thus, many new talents are able to enter the public sphere.

As behavioural deviations are tolerated in him, the genius takes on the role of the avant-garde. In the light of the great things the geniuses have achieved, the applauding bourgeoisie accepts the fact that with their libertinism they call into question the foundation of middle-class decency. Many geniuses become pioneers of innovative lifestyles and point out the way to a new stage of freedom. What is permitted to the genius is adopted with some hesitation by others who aspire to avant-gardistic status. They spread their message as harbingers of the destruction of middle-class morality.

In this and certain other ways, however, the phenomenon of the genius paves the way for systemic consciousness. With the increasing affluence and more and more people gaining access to education, various talents develop in the spheres of art, entertainment, and sports, until almost every sector of human activity has its geniuses: brilliant journalists or actors, stockbrokers or pizza bakers. If the multitude of geniuses becomes unwieldy, so that their achievements can only be fully comprehended by the respective sector, the term loses its defining quality of the beacon for the orientation of collective consciousness. In a society in the process of disposing of its own constraining aspects, extraordinary achievements are no longer granted merely to a very fortunate combination of genes but are encouraged on a broader and broader basis. The more fear, the greatest impediment to creativity, decreases within the human soul, the more creative power is set free.

Excursus: The Bourgeoisie

The social class of the bourgeoisie is responsible not only for materialistic but for personalistic consciousness. In both cases, it is its anti-hierarchical power that weakens and breaks the absolutist systems. Already in the urban sphere of early medieval society, freedom becomes the guiding principle of the bourgeoisie – freedom from the arbitrary rule of the nobility, freedom from absolutist tyranny and dilettantism. Within the flexible structure of the urban society, in which individual performance becomes the yardstick for prestige, the concept of freedom can tend towards a universalistic form – although admittedly, inequalities between the classes of the urban society regarding civil rights and liberties will continue to exist for a long time.

The urban community is a community of opportunities. While in the countryside one had to wear the straitjacket of brutal oppression and constraint, city air was liberating – also because the dynamic urban economy created new opportunities for building up wealth. It is then no longer one's birth but one's individual effort as well as the unpredictable dynamics of the market that decide about one's access to material opportunities. The market, which determines the prices, cannot be explained, is not accountable to anybody – a god of his own making, the god of capitalism.

It is no longer birth (a tribal principle of chance) but commercial success as a combination of individual diligence and intelligence on the one hand and the "good-will" of the market (defined by Calvin as proof for divine favour) on the other hand that determines one's social rank.

The double morality of the bourgeoisie is then plain to see: on the one hand, in personalistic consciousness, it wishes and strives to morally raise itself above the aristocratic hierarchical stubbornness by realising the idea of freedom of spirit; on the other hand, its economic basis is still firmly locked into materialistic consciousness. The function assigned to art by the capitalist bourgeoisie – namely to reconcile these two aspects – has never completely been fulfilled. Art, after all, can never be made to serve one stage of consciousness exclusively, as it is connected to the highest level, by which it is nourished. For a long time, a capitalist could by day overtax his employees and contribute to the destruction of entire colonial cultures and of nature doing his work, and by night suppress his guilt by indulging in the beauty of an opera, deeming himself a sophisticated, noble, chosen human being.

This cynicism in bourgeois consciousness may have been what caused many artists to break with convention and explore more abstract avenues of expression, in the hope of preventing that their art be made to serve bourgeois self-glorification. The bourgeoisie despairs of modern ("degenerate") art, wherein it experiences the limits to its own narcissism, which even nostalgia cannot save. After all, the bourgeoisie looks toward the future, and to respond to its challenges with productive vigour, it must display economic creativity, which can flourish only if there is artistic creativity as well.

The bourgeoisie-driven revolutions of the 18th and 19th centuries were based on changes caused by the economic processes of early capitalism, which undermined the hierarchical systems of administration. By a combination of materialistic and personalistic elements (the French differentiate between the terms *bourgeois* and *citoyen*), these systems can be brought down. The new order grants both capitalism (the pursuit of private profit) and personalism (civil rights and liberties) a solid basis to start from.

The revolutions also lay out the foundation for a global community – whose concept is at first, however, heavily contaminated with imperialist ideas. The ideals of uninhibited economic progress and freedom to live the life of one's own choosing are admired and imitated as a promising new model around the world.

The citizen of the world (*citoyen*) demands his rights as free individual and allows himself (as *bourgeois*) to relentlessly accumulate wealth. But materialistic greed cannot be celebrated limitlessly. Therefore, the hierarchical imbalance of power, which in the mainlands of the European empires was either triumphantly levelled or at least somewhat curtailed (e.g. via the separation of powers), is transferred to the rest of the world. Then we arrive at the paradoxical situation where liberty enjoyed in Europe (colonial or post-colonial) is part-financed through economic and political tyranny over regions outside it.

Thus, again, the tacit bourgeois ambivalence between economic rationality and personal self-discovery is betrayed. We may conclude that the bourgeoisie is rather inapt to serve as the class responsible for the succeeding stage of consciousness.

Ideology and Religion

Stage five is still governed by ideologies – different value systems, manifesting as formulated edifices of ideas about how to and how not to organise the society, motivated by deep-seated fears, with good and evil as opposite poles. Conservatism, liberalism, nationalism and socialism, to name but a few major ideologies, influence us to this day in word and thought, structuring the political scene with their blinkered attitudes.

At stage six, ideologies are no longer tenable, as their one-sided nature and devastating social consequences have become apparent. To every ideology there is a counter-ideology, and one ideology strictly isolates itself from its counter-part so as to make an impression of coherence. Attitudes such as, "my way and no other!" are offspring of a personalistic perspective and cannot survive in the face of systemic criteria. Ideologies always represent the interests of a certain party and can therefore not serve to resolve conflicts. They may help deepen our understanding for specific social groups and their interests; apart from that, they are useless.

For instance, a radical form of feminism that asserts that the biological differences between men and women should have no social consequences (i.e. none whatsoever!), cannot solve the problem of the oppression of women. Our (biological) sexual identity can never completely be absolved from the way we think, talk and act, as if we were made up of two separate beings – a biological and a social-spiritual one –, which did not or should not have anything to do with each other. It is in acknowledging the differences between men and women in terms of biological dispositions as well as social and psychological inclinations that we can pave the way for an improved culture of communication and for a fair distribution of opportunities and responsibilities.

The guiding star in the personalistic war against the hierarchical apparatus and the forces of machines is freedom of will. "Man is ... free, and were he born in shackles". Schiller's utterance may be understood as the motto of personalistic consciousness. If we live according to the principle of personal freedom, our awareness of our true identity will increase. By acting of our own accord, we make of ourselves what we are. "Become what you are": through the choices and actions in your life develop into the person that is authentically you. Since the late 18th century, elaborate paedagogical concepts have pointed out an alternative to bureaucratically administered and materialistically degenerated education: it is one's authentic character that should be developed.

The freedom that personalistic consciousness brought helped build up an enormous creative potential and variety in the arts, in the economy, and in science, but also led to a hypertrophy and an over-glorification of the idea of freedom and those embodying it.

One of the tragic misunderstandings in personalistic consciousness is caused by attaching its idea of freedom to the person as highest authority, so that every infringement of individual freedom is interpreted as a return to hierarchical oppression and is therefore fought. The fiction of the august personality, soon to be demasked by psychology as narcissist ego, must be upheld at any cost, so as not to jeopardize the acquisitions of this progressive course. The "great" political (mis-)leaders of the 20th century, from Mussolini to Pol Pot, who abused their freedom of will to command bureaucratically administered mass murders, are the distorted image of unbridled personalism.

Thus, well into the 20th century, the fact was overlooked – and remains unrecognised to this day – that the achievements of personalistic consciousness are not lost if they are embedded in systemic contexts, wherein they are relativized, and eventually fade into the background in holistic consciousness. When the ego as a hotchpotch of chronic fears loses its central importance, the person, too, must leave its prominent position. Once the personality cult has been abandoned, it becomes easier also to part with the dogma of freedom of will, as holistic thought and experience suggest.

As an internal, guiding authority for free will, human conscience is given a very prominent role. At preceding stages of consciousness, its full force was largely unknown: it is at the personalistic stage where the conscience develops to its fullest. In the course of evolution, it has appeared in various guises: as the internalised tribal rule with the power to exterminate the offender; as guilt felt by the hero on the evening after the battle; as differentiation into pragmatic conduct towards betters and subordinates on the one hand and moral conduct towards peers on the other hand; and as authority for self-justification in materialism. In Immanuel Kant's moral philosophy, legality and morality are distinguished in clear terms; and the priority in one's life, according to Kant, should be for the latter of the two, namely for recognising and obeying the laws of morality, which are now subject to examination by the mind.

Defined by conscience and freedom of will, personalistic consciousness presents the issue of the afterlife in a new light. It is not satisfied with the reductionisms of materialism. Turning inside and seeing through to the emptiness and cruelty at the core of the capitalist economy, it is eager to transcend the material world. Human consciousness, however, can no longer be contented with the traditional religious communities and their formulae of transcendence. All the reformers of the church refer to such personal experiences. Martin Luther, for instance, experienced the comprising power and the human dependency on mercy in the middle of a storm. Motivated by his experience, he turns against the hierarchical apparatus of power of the Catholic Church. He fails to reform the institution and cannot prevent the movement he first initiated from getting out of hand and establishing its own apparatus of power. The separatist tendencies within the church continue, and many other Christian denominations are promulgated.

One of the consequences of this individualisation of religion is thus the splitting up of Christianity into a number of different churches, which leads to the enlightened concept of tolerance that, "everyone find salvation in his own way" (Friedrich II. of Prussia). In the face of the numerous options of religious denomination, a choice must be made. Or, as a logical extension to this form of individualisation: everyone founds his own church.

At least, personalistic consciousness cannot ignore the crucial question asked by the character Margaret in Goethe's Faust, "How do you feel about religion?". Personalistic consciousness must relate to the whole, as it feels separated from it and can no longer ignore this sense of separation or drown it in materialistic excess. It seeks to open up, and all attempts made in this consciousness lead to unknown territory. At some moments, our efforts will indeed take us to the universalistic plane of consciousness. They are moments of peak experiences of encounters with nature, art or mysticism. But if these experiences are to become the foundation of a new stage of evolution, they must first be widened and stabilised.

The Power of Knowledge and the Endless Train of Questions

Personalistic consciousness does not embrace any form of solipsism; its intention is not to consider the individual in isolation. Many "great" people do indeed appear under its banner as single artists and scientists, and it does seem that it was these individuals that initiated all the key developments in the last few centuries. We tend to forget that those people owe greatly to those that went before them, whose ideas they studied, adopted, and reformulated. This is because the myth of the hero has been mesmerized, generalised and romanticised by bourgeois society. The bourgeoisie wants to overcome its relative insignificance and the monotony of economic everyday life by projecting its values onto the genius.

Oftentimes, the "great" are very good at communicating and are wont to exchange ideas with others. They surround themselves with peers and followers and found schools. In front of an audience, they display superb rhetoric skills, orally or in writing. Happily, they claim possession of the products of their mind. They have realised that knowledge is power, that the ownership of information brings greater influence and insights even than access to financial and bureaucratic resources. They, however, have not yet found out the secret of knowledge: if information is consumed, i.e. shared, it does not decrease like physical matter but grows.

The scientist is one of the prototypes of personalistic consciousness. He is the member of a new "tribe", the scientific community. To this class, he owes his intellectual career, his legitimation and his reputation. This community has given rise to an important paradigm that is now widely acknowledged. In our day, the scientific mode of establishing the truth is held to be the most trustworthy of all and has taken the place of authority formerly held by priests and politicians. Thus, the scientist takes a most prestigious position in society.

This paradigm is grounded in personalistic consciousness: every scientific finding should be such as can be verified by any other person. If, for instance, a scientist asserts that planet Jupiter has x moons, any other person who explores the moons of Jupiter applying the appropriate tools and calculations should arrive at the same result.

Thus, one's claim to truth is no longer based on power (those who have power are right) but universal consensus, which is not the exclusive property of a single person or a privileged class. Things that all people can recognise as the truth if they go by their personal experiences and exercise reason, must indeed be true. Dogmas, which evade intersubjective examination, are dethroned and fall into disrepute.

The limits to this scientific criterion for truth become apparent where individual experiences as such make a claim to truth but just cannot be shared by all individuals. Scientists dote on sensory experiences and mathematically logical thinking, assuming that the responsible mechanisms of the mind are identical with us all in so far as our experiences and interpretations are wholly independent of our personality.

This survey, for instance, cannot make a claim to truth supported by the sort of intersubjectivity mentioned above. Much of what is postulated here cannot be reproduced directly via sensory experiences. The insights this text is based on are only to a small part founded in conventional logic. The reader may arrive at different conclusions or regard other connections as more important than are discussed here. Nevertheless, I hope that in reading this book you will gain insights grounded in a deeper truth than the objectivity of conventional scientific procedures can convey.

Science may be capable of establishing pathways to all levels of consciousness, but it cannot venture the step onto the final plane of consciousness. This step requires the courage to rely on one's own intuition, which is not accessible to scientific portrayal.

Systemic thinking shakes the scientific world view. Understanding in a systemic sense is always relative: every scientist has a certain position he cannot abandon. The findings of quantum physics break the limits of the space-time continuum, which are required by the senses to provide relevant data. They also point beyond the limits of logic, whose premise is that A must always be A and cannot be anything else.

The power of the classical scientific paradigm was thus restricted to a limited intellectual area; but the universalistic criterion continued to be the guiding star in all further scientific enterprises. The systemic approach with its constructivist features also holds a place in the kingdom of science for all the younger fields bordering on physics.

The social sciences and humanities, whose principles follow other regularities, have always represented quite a contrast to the "solid" natural sciences with their "hard facts". The hermeneutic methods of social sciences and humanities, whose aim is to understand rather than measure the world, generate culturally dependent knowledge and require other criteria. From a systemic viewpoint, they are equal to any other form of scientific research.

Nature

This enables a novel relation to nature, which is connected to the enthusiasm of rediscovery after the alienation from nature in materialism. Nature is experienced as great hoard of the analogous in strong contrast to the empire of figures. Thus, the mystical and inexplicable, the chaotic and the uncanny are restored to the human conscious.

The portrayal of nature in Romanticism exposes a mystified concept of it, whose underlying idea is that of refuge from the world of machines. Yet this concept represents a feeble challenge to the overwhelming power of materialism. But this dialectic will be levelled as soon as it becomes apparent what the logic of materialism will eventually lead to, namely the destruction of life itself. Then, nature again positions itself as a challenging opposition to a one-dimensional orientation of growth; then systems must be introduced that can encompass and respect both dimensions.

The revaluation of nature is just one among many examples for the destruction of the standards that take place in a society gone personalistic. Now women, too, demand what has been denied to them since the days of individualistic hero-worship. The economic equalisation, which occurred through the embracing of the numerical principle of capitalism, has an influence on sexual power relations. In the face of women's successes in various professional sectors, it becomes harder and harder to justify men's privileged position. The personalistic principle proves superior to the hierarchical strategy of assessment, where any kind of hegemonial relation is justified on the grounds of natural differences. Nature, after all, does not assess: it allows differences to exist side by side, like all the flowers on a meadow, which cannot be played off against one another but deserve equal respect, even though they appear in different forms and colours.

Personalistic consciousness sees through the lies of the hierarchical systems and takes a critical view. The unique individual cannot be tied down to a concept, and categorisations such as, "All women are x and all men are y" have no more weight in an argument in the face of this new order of reason. Power and leadership have to be legitimized before this personalistic reason. They are morally condemned and are dismissed, first in the minds of people and later concrete reality. Eventually, all unjust systems that have not emancipated themselves from their hierarchical origins are destroyed.

One of these unjust systems is that which grants men and women unequal access to professional opportunities. As soon as the narrow view employed here is abandoned, the process of social evolution grows in creative power.

With the emancipation of fringe groups and subcultures, it is similar. Every group identity, whether it is formed by sexual orientation, cultural interest, or ethnic origin, must make an original contribution to the cultural network. It is the fear of anarchy inherent in the hierarchical system that prohibits, denies, persecutes, or eradicates whatever does not fit into the superimposed concept of society. The inner progress of the evolution of consciousness lacks them both: the powers which are invested in oppression and the powers which are destroyed by oppression.

At the stage of personalistic consciousness, such fringe groups strive for greater acknowledgement in the public sphere, demanding equal rights. The personalistic principle is in favour of these developments, and so a variety of cultural views and ways of living pass from the marginal shade into the light of broad public recognition to contribute new ideas and visions. This results in the imperative that what has hitherto been put at a disadvantage be no longer excluded or discriminated against but integrated into society, encouraged and supported.

The fear of anarchy, which stands in the way of such processes of emancipation and integration, results from the central strife of hierarchical consciousness to curtail individual arbitrariness. All things different must be subjected to rigid mechanisms of control, because they are seen as a challenge to the existing balance of power. Therefore, in absolutist systems certain religious groups are banned, persecuted and driven out – only to contribute essential works in the places where they settle instead. Although many of these communities do not aspire to political power, they are alleged to do so and are fought as political opponents. Obsession for power, as shared by individualistic and hierarchical consciousness, is projected onto all alien groups, until the paranoia rises to a point where the whole system is destroyed by its own absurdity. Unfortunately, in many cases the system will not collapse before its main protagonists perish: Stalinism and fascism have shown this all too plainly.

The thirst for knowledge spurs critical thinking. Everything that people take for granted, every habit, every starting point is questioned. Socrates pestered his contemporaries with his questions about what they meant by what they were saying. Immanuel Kant wrote three critiques on his three main questions: what can I know, what should I do, and what may I hope for? Friedrich Nietzsche, "philosophising with a hammer", dissected and unmasked all-too-human hypocritical attitudes. Sigmund Freud effectively undermined people's conviction that their actions were grounded in rationality.

The Problem of Theodizee as Example

One of the issues of personalistic consciousness is the problem of justifying the suffering in the world. If there is a just and benevolent God, then why does He allow for human misery? Many ideas have been put forward in answer to this question, from the assertion that such a God cannot exist, to the claim that the question can never be answered comprehensibly and that the divine mystery is revealed in precisely in this fact. The idea of Karma has been tried (people suffer because they caused suffering in previous lives – Hinduism) as well as that of the hidden God whose intentions must remain a mystery (*deus absconditus* – Martin Luther). Augustin defined evil as lack of goodness, while Zarathustra spoke of two equally powerful forces of good and evil. The deists suggested that after Creation God ceased to interfere in the fate of the world and can therefore not be blamed for its evils.

Personalistic consciousness exults in the inexhaustibility of individuality: here it hits a limit. One opinion opposes the other and there is no one authority that could sort everything out. And the habit of questioning is taken up again and is carried on to infinity. The train of questions often ends in resignation and depression or leads to blind, scornful action.

When saying in his *Tractatus* that every question already entails the answer, Wittgenstein refers the personalistic inquirer to the systemic plane. There the main focus is not on questions and answers but on the context in which certain questions make sense. The answer is in the context, not in something completely new that is made accessible by asking a question. Every question rather serves to define the boundaries within which a meaningful answer can be given.

> "Most propositions and questions, that have been written about philosophical matters, are not false, but senseless. We cannot, therefore, answer questions of this kind at all, but only state their senselessness." (Tractatus 4.003)

In our model, Wittgenstein's utilisation of "pointless" would translate as "belonging to a previous stage". At the systemic stage, people can ask questions only within the framework of the system they are in. Since God is already defined as something outside the system of mankind, a question as to His motives cannot be answered and is therefore pointless.

> "For an answer which cannot be expressed the question too cannot be expressed. The *riddle* does not exist. If a question can be put at all, then it can also be answered." (Tractatus 6.5)

> "The real discovery is the one that makes me capable of stopping doing philosophy when I want to.— The one that gives philosophy peace, so that it is no longer tormented by questions which bring itself in question." (Philosophical Investigations 133)

The attitude of holistic consciousness to the problem of theodizee is one of the subjects of the next chapter but one.

Social Structures in Personalistic Consciousness

The idea of using the word "partnership" to denote "love relationship" grew out of personalistic consciousness. It was transferred from the world of business to the sphere of relationships. For many enterprises and projects, you need partners; when those enterprises and projects are over, so is the partnership. Mutual reliability is grounded in a common cause, not in deeper interest in the other person. This is a mortgage that personalism inherited from materialism.

In post-tribal communities, sexual relationships were subject to strict regulations that had to do with the structure of peasant communities. The necessary division of labour on the farm was transferred to relationships. A man and a woman depended on each other and were tied to each other. Individual demands were subjugated to the economic pressures. The need to survive under the meanest conditions required people to set priorities, and their private life was not one of them. And the hierarchy was fixed according to patriarchal guidelines: the Austrian civil code of 1812 to 1976, for instance, defined the man as head of the family.

In the wake of materialism was born a form of economy that ensured the survival of the masses and gave more and more people access to goods and services formerly reserved exclusively for the aristocracy. The economic developments also affected the quality of relationships. Emotional needs are given a voice; the issue of romantic love, formerly the theme of aristocratic romances and courtly intrigues, begins to transcend all boundaries of class.

The prevalent questions are now: Is there enough love? Is my relationship pleasant and fulfilling? If the answer is no, there is the possibility of separating. Due to the thriving economy, the survival of the married individuals does not depend on their staying together. A notion like, "Till death do you part" gradually loses its connotation of naturalness. The emotional demands of personalistic consciousness put every partnership to the test, turning every relationship into a test-partnership.

In the personalistic formulation of the question of love, there is still a materialistic undertone. This is inherent both in the desire for more for fear of losing out, and in the tendency of applying the digital principle of measurement to the world of feelings. Do you love me enough, and to what scale? Compared with what?

The addictive pattern of materialism, which at the previous stage was directed toward material objects, is now transferred to love relationships. The progress is in the partial reversal of the process of alienation from nature: now it is people, i.e. living beings, who become the objects of desire. The addictive character that defines the romantic form of sexual relationships (cf. the epic entanglement of Tristan and Isolde) has a disastrous influence on the course of the rearrangement of relationships in connection with personalistic consciousness.

The French saying has it that, "Love is the child of liberty". Yet romantic addiction, as it were, takes love for a prisoner. Happiness depends on the success of relationships; if they go wrong, there is desperation. The lover of the personalistic plane has learnt that happiness is not to be looked for in the world of material objects but often fails in her attempts to find her one and true love in human form. Many of the violent dramas of our day tie in with this issue. In many Western countries, most violent and murderous deeds are connected with ill-fated or refused love.

Psychology, the offspring of personalistic consciousness, investigates more and more into the subject of love, realising that the immoderate demands partners place on each other go back to the unfulfilled needs of love in their childhood. The parental love and affection the individual missed in his childhood he will later demand of his partner. This is why so many relationships fail. Personalistic sensitivity, the openness to the dark corners of the soul and the naming of unfulfilled needs shake the traditional foundations of long-term relationships and cause many writers to discuss the crisis of the institution of marriage.

The over-taxation of the personalistic individual with relationships overloaded with emotions and expectations points to another limit of this form of consciousness. It is therefore in the areas of couple and family therapy that systemic approaches are developed and for the time appreciated outside the scientific disciplines.

Of course, it is not only love relationships that need a new framework. At this stage, groups are formed that strive to break out of the confines of their family circle, groups of heroes (and their descendants, the fraternities and paramilitary units), groups ordered according to social rank, as well as interest and pressure groups. Characteristically at this stage, groups are no longer formed on the basis of descent or materialistic purpose. Personalistic fellowship is based on shared world views, i.e. on shared interpretations of personal orientation. The groups are joined voluntarily and mostly for a limited temporal space, for merely a phase in one's journey through life. We are talking about loose communities rather than tight bodies, which are open to everyone but less durable or binding. The historical line runs from the salons of the 18th-century bourgeoisie to the communes and alternative domestic communities of our day.

Common ideals are the binding factors within these communities, while individual differences of interpretation may lead to separation. In order to ensure their long-term survival, groups need to be able to handle conflicts. Conversation is the characteristic medium within personalistic communities for establishing interactive connections. Members use their language for various communicative purposes. In the context of personalistic consciousness, a specific mode of verbal communication evolves: the dialogue. In Martin Buber's definition, the participants of a dialogue respect each other's individuality and work to create a common sphere of connection, in which both of them feel accepted and safe. They open up both to each other and to the depths of their own soul. They learn new things about themselves and experience the power of relationships.

The World Wars as Shock for Personalistic Consciousness

19th-century Europe can be described as the heyday of personalistic consciousness. In the face of new breakthroughs in the economic, technological, scientific and medical fields, bourgeois society becomes obsessed with the idea of progress and rejoices in its increasing wealth of goods and creativity. The euphoria of progress, however, is buried on the battlefields of World War One. The ideals of humanity appear hollow and impotent in the face of a destructive dynamic triggered by an unfortunate blend of components from all stages previous. The intellectual climate is determined by this crisis of human identity after the fall of personalistic idealism. Straightforward thinking and faith in inner progress are now obsolete and regarded as naive. The lack of models of the evolution of consciousness leaves only a narrow path between magnificence of mind and self-destruction.

The trauma of two world wars, which comprises millions of individual traumatisations, runs through all cultural circles the world over. National Socialism showed how easy it can be to disempower all the ideals of humanity and how small the voice of personalistic reason becomes once unfulfilled needs from earlier stages of consciousness have effectively been channelled and instrumentalised in the masses. Furthermore, after the fall of the worst regimes ever known to man, the concepts of total war and politically organised genocide was exported from Europe to the rest of the world. Personalistic consciousness could not cope with this shock and painfully witnessed its own hubris.

Problems for the Transition from Stage Five to Six

The individual body-soul complex is a closed system with clear boundaries. Although it may permanently interact with many other systems, we are often not aware of these intersubjective processes, especially when under stress. Then our unconscious survival pattern is activated, aimed at keeping the organism from harm. Thus, a perspective of rigid seclusion is established, which we tend to take for reality.

This view is further supported by our perception being determined by our senses. Although we are capable of imagining what a system is like we will not find it easy to actually come to grips with it unless we experience it by our senses. When in doubt, we will always trust our senses. Thus, we are stuck with the subject-object perspective.

That's the heart of personalistic consciousness – thinking in individualities: I am what I am – I am the way I am. This is me in a nutshell. The external world is different, strange, unknown; contact is possible but not obligatory. I am an individual, and I laugh and cry solely for myself.

Yet all along the systemic aspect of the human soul influences us subtly. Only if we expand our mind can we become aware of this strong influence. To do so, we must abandon many of the ideas we have hitherto been entertaining, which is not an easy task.

When systemic consciousness is growing strong inside our soul, we may feel a sense of relief. This, however, does not mean that we are necessarily willing to forsake the sensations of autonomy and freedom conveyed by personalistic consciousness. The mere thought of being tied to a powerful system can provoke feelings of restriction and confinement.

Our Inner Imprintings of the Personalistic Stage

The questioning of pre-set structures is characteristic of this stage. Adolescents cast doubt on everything taken as a matter of course. They reflect on the issues of their time. What is my personal opinion of the current problems of society? How do I feel about religion? Which ideas are worth embracing? Which should I avoid? What do I want to stand up for?

All these questions stand in lieu of the major question: Who am I? I can be happy only if I know myself and trust myself. What is my goal in life? I must take matters into my own hands and see what life brings. This is the phase of radical self-reflection, which is in itself a precondition for the evolution of an adult identity.

How can we identify the patterns we adopted in the fifth phase of the evolution of consciousness? Let us consider the fears, fixations, and resources stemming from this specific stage in our past.

Characteristic Fears:

- Fear of not living one's life to the fullest, of making too little of it (If I don't seize my chances and use my talents, life will pass me by)
- Fear of being average and dull (I have no real profile, I'm like all the others, I have no style)
- Fear of not being appreciated the way one is (people don't see who I really am and what my potential is)
- Fear of missing something important (if I don't take all the opportunities I will get and make the most of every moment, will I feel alive?)

Negative Fixations:

- Vanity, narcissist inclinations (the vain self-admirer)
- Feelings of inferiority and debasement of oneself (the mouse)
- Overestimation of feelings and passion (the hysterical drama king)
- Disdain of simple or practical actions (the prissy princess)

Resources:

- Confidence in one's individuality
- Appreciation of personal communication
- Understanding for the diversity of human emotions and their importance in life
- Self-confidence and self-worth
- Creativity, artistic ambition

Exercises

Pride

purpose: gaining a better understanding of the meaning of pride and improving one's attitude towards it

indications: other people's accusation of arrogance; "allergic" reactions to arrogant people

We are all no strangers to pride, which might be referred to as the most extreme form of self-confidence ("Pride is the emotional certainty of one's own importance" - Fernando Pessoa). We can exaggerate expression of self-confidence to lift ourselves above others. On the other hand, if we debase or reject this attitude too much, we will end up in its shadow, being proud of not being proud.

Instructions: Take a piece of paper and divide it into two columns. In the left column, write down all the things you are proud of in your life. In the right column, jot down all the things you are not proud of. Leave a little space under every point you mention. Then fill those blanks with notes on what you think you have learnt from each respective item.

Now close your eyes: imagine that one day you will have to let go of all that you are proud of. Witness any feeling that's coming up. How important are to you the things you have achieved? What would remain if you had to forsake all that?

Enter the heart, the innermost core of your being. In this place, are you really dependent on what you have achieved, or on the judgment you or other people have passed about yourself? Or is it a place where you can feel free to be just the way you are, no matter what you have or have not achieved, or what the future holds? A place where you are invaluable, where nothing you have accomplished or in which you have failed is significant for your own worth.

Now imagine doing what you always do, but with the feeling that everything you are proud of is suddenly trivial and that all you are doing, no matter if common or out of the ordinary, is of equal value. How does this make you feel? Let your breath flow freely – easefully – until you are able to stay calm when imagining it.

Creativity

purpose: mobilising one's potential

indications: lack of initiative and creativity

Instructions: What are your special talents? You don't have to compete with stars: identify your area of potential power where you can achieve and create great things. It can be inconspicuous activities like setting the table, arranging flowers, showing stamina at a hiking tour, coming up with hilarious one-liners, singing songs ... It can be visions you have in your head, of projects that you keep postponing, that you may not think yourself capable of realising. A new line of work? A new hobby? Writing a novel? Painting a picture? Recall the ideas you had long ago and that you forsook, or think of the ones that you have been carrying around with you for ages. What can you do to finally realise them?

Choose an idea or project that fascinates or interests you. Can you sense feelings of motivation when you think of it? How would it feel if you had realised the project? Let the image of your dream come true arise in your mind's eye; feel the power emanating from it. It is your personal creative power, and you can use it to reach your goal.

Qualities

purpose: arriving at the insight that we live in a world of wonders

indications: black moods, feelings of emptiness and boredom

Instructions: What qualities are there in your life (and don't think about your bank account)? What aspects are there in your life that you appreciate for their beauty, sublimity, or uniqueness?

Take your time looking at a flower, and do not stop when you think you have seen everything. Look out for details, subtleties and nuances you have never noticed before. And see the flower as a perfect whole. As you look at the flower, take care not to think about the future or the past: stay in the moment.

Now take a look at another object, maybe something less pretty, like a kitchen tool. Can you look at this object from the same angle as from which you looked at the flower?

If you do this exercise, you may learn to see the wealth of qualities around you. There is so much for you to discover here. So why be bored?

Your Part in Life

purpose: gaining clarity about one's own life

indications: doubts about oneself, dissatisfaction in one's daily life and job

Instructions: Close your eyes, take a few deep breaths and relax while breathing out.

Ask yourself the question: what is the highest goal in my life? In your mind's eye, create an image, an internal symbol. This image appears in bright and shiny colours. In the background, there is music sounding to it. Deeply inhale the power of this image, and assign to the image a specific location in your body.

In case you want to put greater effort into this purpose: what could you change in your life? How would it feel if you made the change? What could help you in doing so?

This exercise is to help you gain a deeper understanding of the part you are meant to play in this world and how much of it you are actually performing. You are free to decide whether or not to take it more seriously.

* * *

You are unique as the person you are. Greater assurance of this can grow from knowing the personalistic plane. You can use your personalistic resources to detach yourself from unjustified expectations and prejudices other people trouble you with. You will see your life as a series of evolutionary steps, every single one of them bearing the mark of self-expression. Along the journey, your individual task will reveal itself to you in success and failure alike. You will see how with every new experience you will rise to even greater maturity.

Stage 6: Systemic Consciousness – Man in the World of Networks

Men are disturbed, not by things, but by the principles and notions which they form concerning things.

(Epictetus, Enchiridion 5)

The robbed that smiles steals something from the thief.

(William Shakespeare, Othello)

Key aspects:
complex thinking, relationships instead of positions, processes instead of qualities, relativism and post-modern understanding of culture, fear of losing control

> *John closed his briefcase and looked at his watch. Still half an hour left until the next meeting. He would go by foot: he wanted to feel his muscles, as there wouldn't be time for jogging within the next few days. Also, it would be good for his carbon footprint.*
>
> *Crossing the inner city, he was going to have three talks. He was to bring N. and S. together, as both these two had developed valuable ideas for the implementation of new solar technologies in public institutions. That would fit in well with the overall strategy of his organisation. He was to inform T. on the outcome of the meeting; and maybe Karabaya could tell him if the children, who had flown off for their social project in Latin America, had phoned home. Also, he should tell her that L. from the marketing agency would be coming for dinner at the Thai restaurant and that she could not yet say for sure if her husband would be joining them as well.*
>
> *There was a lot to do, but on a day like today, John was confident that everything can fit together in a harmonious way, as if connected by an invisible web of fine strings. This idea took all the pressure on the inside.*

Life in Larger, Flexible Contexts

Historically speaking, the world founded in the ideals of personalistic reason was at an end in mid-twentieth century and had to admit to its failure. Two abhorring world wars showed the insufficiencies of a world order based on subjective principles. There was an imbalance between the exorbitant technological developments that had led to the construction of weapons for mass destruction, and the lack of a moral authority that could successfully keep their madness in check. Enlightened thought had come up against a boundary it could not penetrate. Late Enlightenment therefore sways between negative dialectics and utter dismay about the failure of reason to avoid the abyss of human malice.

A new way of thinking capable of overcoming the dangers of personalistic egotism is employed, manifesting in the form of systemic models and concepts. Oriented at technological metaphorism, this new way of interpreting the world pushes forward into the jungle of modern life-styles.

It was art that helped pave the way for such developments. At the beginning of the 20th century, the musical avant-garde departed from the idea of tonal structures. No one note should be privileged amongst the others in representing the keynote. In the world of music, there should be no primate: all notes should be equal. The question how the respective notes relate to one another becomes more important than the individual qualities of notes. The personalistic listener, who expects to find central and indispensable points of reference in the sequence of notes, feels disappointed and offended by the new music.

Systemic Thinking and Constructivism

The novel view of the world is no longer applied to given principles such as that of logic or that of linguistic structures: even the premises are relativized. The systemic approach follows along these lines. Although any way of thinking, any form of attitude, any mode of reflection can be employed, its validity is restricted to the scope of the respective system. Thus, the idea of absolute reason, which represents a safe crucial point in a world of transient phenomena, is abandoned. Relativity, which, likewise at the beginning of the 20th century, had undermined the theoretical basis of classical physics, is applied to all methodologies.

Systemic thinking, then, is not about arriving at a right point of view and revolutionising the world from that particular position. Instead, it is important to be able to adopt as many positions as possible and experience their respective qualities. Only then can we acknowledge the manifold interactions that make up the network of reality. The main focus is thus not on the different elements but on their relations. It is a dynamic world view that does not ask for absolute truths but refers to relative, temporary insights. Pragmatism replaces dogmatism, and one-dimensionality makes way for versatility.

If the main focus is on relations, on what happens in between, instead of the entities themselves, then the systemic world view takes an even greater distance from material objects than the personalistic one. Our access to the meaning of an entity does not depend just on whether we perceive it but also on the way we perceive it. As Wittgenstein said,

> If good or bad willing changes the world, it can only change the limits of the world, not the facts; not the things that can be expressed in language. In brief, the world must thereby become quite another. It must so to speak wax or wane as a whole. The world of the happy is quite another than that of the unhappy.
> (Tractatus 6.43)

The truth about the world is thus made accessible not by the world itself (i.e. the facts, objects and processes) but by the right attitude of those examining it. There is no reality as such, and if there were, it would not make sense to talk of it. But there are ways of representing reality, which lend meaning to it, no matter if this meaning can be expressed in words.

Wittgenstein may have given less thought to the problem of the sources of happiness and unhappiness: but it his philosophy set clear boundaries both to materialistic and personalistic consciousness, which made him a precursory figure in the arrival of systemic consciousness. His theory of language-games, too, is an important contribution to the social implementation of systemic consciousness.

The Constructivist Approach

What is central to the systemic view of reality is the constructivist approach. According to constructivism, whatever position is adopted, it is always relative. It is a point on a wilfully drawn map, and the location in the real world that this point corresponds to does not exist except in relation to those relating to it.

According to constructivism, all positions are equally valid, as there is no position from which it could be judged that one position is better than another. Looking at the world from a certain perspective, we may appreciate some positions more than others. But this preference is not of objective relevance: it is relevant only for us and for this moment. It does not tell us anything about whether one position is better than another.

If I don't see the orange elephant that my neighbour claims to see, then my perception is different from his, but not "better". If we talk about our views, we establish a new, communicative reality, in which we may agree that one of us sees the orange elephant and the other does not.

According to systemic consciousness, one is always right – subjectively speaking. This is the essence of constructivism, arguing an attitude of acceptance towards everyone and everything, including ourselves.

Constructivism may sound convincing and simple in theory, but its practical application requires constant verification. Often we make assumptions about reality that we prematurely think of as true. What we tend to forget is that assumptions formulated from our limited subjective viewpoint represent models of reality – at best. Thus, it takes enormous flexibility and an inexhaustible learning ability to sustain systemic consciousness.

What we will gain is a chance for breaking free from the narrow ideas of the Ego: nothing is necessarily as we expect it to be. We will learn to accept things the way they present themselves to us, to change what should be changed, and to in turn accept the fruits of our efforts, no matter how they turn out.

Also, we will come to realise that holding on to our own viewpoint without respecting the position of another may decelerate the positive evolutionary process of a system. There is an urge within the system for constant improvement, a drive that forces people to shelve their individual interests for the sake of a common goal of success, from which they could all benefit.

As authority of construction and centre of reality, however, the Ego persists. It may even have the presumption to claim authorship of everything around it, confusing the system itself with the total of its projections. Rational presence of mind or new philosophical ideas are not enough to break the shackles of the Ego: it is primarily through inner work and personal development reaching far into the depths of the dark places of the soul that we achieve their destruction.

On the path to systemic consciousness, we must confront many of our fears. Prejudices, stereotypes, schematic forms of judgement, dogmas, theoretical axioms, and all species of religious fundamentalism, so central to the keeping of the status quo of previous stages, must be reassessed as relative and conditional. Such contents of consciousness and collective belief systems grew from attempts at controlling certain fears and the unpredictabilities of life. This shows that the step from to systemic consciousness from a previous stage cannot be taken before a certain level of fearlessness has been reached. Some sense of security that was formerly regarded as a matter of course must now be renunciated.

Up to now, every time people entered a new stage of consciousness, their fears did not decrease to a considerable extent, appearing in other guises rather than actually abating. People were driven mainly by the fears that resulted from the objective predicaments of each respective stage and were reinforced subjectively due to an increasing internalisation of these situations.

Systemic consciousness, on the other hand, asks of its protagonists that they break free from many of their fear-driven inner limitations; only then may they participate. Such limitations should no longer serve as the main motivators for their actions, and they are supposed be capable of shelving their fears to such an extent as they will no longer dominantly interfere with their actions and considerations.

Systems meant to generate productive output must be independent of irrational fears. Fear, no matter how subtle its influence, is like a spanner in the works, preventing ideal solutions for problems in social networks, organisations, and institutions.

The personalistic stage paves the way for such developments by turning the fear of the individual into a central theme (cf. Kierkegaard) and exploring ways of escaping from their clutches (cf. the invention of psychoanalysis). Thus, people learn to tell fear-driven actions from fear-free ones: and this ability is one of the qualifications it takes to gain entry to the systemic stage. The systemic mind-set can function well only when fear has been reduced considerably. However, it is only in a state of holistic consciousness that fear disappears entirely from the inner landscape.

One of the fears characteristic of the systemic stage in particular is the fear of globalisation. What we mean by this is neither the widespread fear in developed countries of the outsourcing of jobs into countries with a low-wage economy nor the fear in less developed countries of further impoverishment and marginalisation. At this stage of consciousness, the feeling that everything is connected with everything increases with the importance of systemic thinking to the individual mind and society. Human suffering anywhere in the world, after a natural disaster or in the continuous stress of struggling for survival, no longer exists only "over there" but besets the world of plenty as a shadow.

How can we meet the demands of global solidarity when the world's misery seems almost infinite? People in need can be encountered in the streets, on long-distance trips, through the media and when we look inside our heart to reflect on the state of humanity. If from a systemic point of view there is no difference between those who live close to us and those who live far away, then I cannot possibly be more ready to support the victims of the earthquake in land A than the flood victims in land B. Should I, then, abandon all attitudes of compassion and solidarity because it is far beyond me to save the whole world and just helping some would be unfair to the others who were left out?

Systemic consciousness can help us to moderate our claims and remain capable of acting. The idea that the world's misery and its termination are my responsibility belongs to personalistic consciousness. The personalistic stage is where we long for immeasurable powers, for miracle-working personalities capable of saving the entire human race.

As soon as we see the world as infinite system of systems we can let go of exaggerated claims and expectations. Every situation is woven into various different systems. Mind and action of individual members of a system are limited, and they cannot take care of what is out of their reach. Other systems will take care of that.

The individual then demands of herself only to assume an attitude of servitude and make the best her potential. The less there is of inner or collective fear, the greater is the potential for constructive and compassionate deeds. Then it can longer be the chore of a single individual to alleviate the suffering of all: then the force for good is in effect wherever possible.

Systemic consciousness radically questions the traditional concept of reality (i.e. that reality is made of clearly defined objects). The constructivist concept of reality is argued in scientific terms and is part of the epistemological line of development of modern philosophy (which began with Immanuel Kant), representing thus a further development of ideas from the personalistic stage.

In the olden days, Hinduist and Buddhist philosophy had already questioned the "reality" of reality and, by systematically doubting the naivety of perception, had thrust open the doors to holistic consciousness. Everything, it was said, which appears reliable in the material world, is in fact evanescent and may pass away anytime. All things, animate or inanimate, must pass. Even our individual self, which we took so great care to nourish and keep from harm, will one day dissolve into thin air.

A Farewell to Habits of Thinking

Every human being prefers those ways of thinking that have always worked for her and that gives her a sense of security. Creating an order in the world so that we may move about in it with some predictability is one of the main functions of the human mind. According to constructivism and systemic consciousness, we can only create models of reality and never get hold of reality itself – postulating universal principles, therefore, does not pertain to us.

One person will say that there is an afterlife, another will claim that there isn't, and yet another will assert that we die to be reborn. One person will say that we have a free will, another person will deny this, while a third party might opine that free will exists only if we believe that it does.

At the stage of systemic consciousness, our traditional views on what is good, just, sublime or beautiful, seem mere models devised by the human mind, and our claim to superior knowledge and wisdom suddenly makes us appear arrogant. And indeed, there is something quite ludicrous about arguing over some topics; I am being reminded of a scene from the film "The Phantom of Liberty" (by Luis Buñuel), where two sword-fighters duel to the death, one of them crying, "God exists", the other, "God does not exist" – as if the existence of God depended on the outcome of the fight. Constructivism, however, is beyond waging religious wars.

And yet, from the point of view of holistic consciousness, which requires no models of reality whatsoever, constructivist thinking is more of a crutch, a state of transition, a remedy for the narrow-mindedness and rigidity of thought of earlier stages.

The order of value assignments is among the casualties of systemic consciousness. Values derive from reality (realism) – that which is good for all elements of a system is considered valuable. They can no longer be grounded in selfish interest and group egotism but must be adapted with flexibility to the requirements of each respective situation.

The systemic stage embraces the best pragmatic models serving to tackle all kinds of problems. A great deal of creativity is now unleashed, as many of the fears and inner limitations have become marginal to people. The playful and flexible quality of this form is capable of serving life in all its aspects.

What is now increasingly required of people is life-long learning, not only in terms of the accumulation of declarative knowledge (i.e. informational knowledge), but also with regard to abilities, attitudes, and ways of thinking. This includes not only the artfulness required for handling the new wonders of technology, but also competences relevant for the social and emotional well-being of a system. These are certainly important if people want to actually reap the benefits of systemic consciousness and actively contribute to its further development.

The process of the evolution of values requires great personal stability, which at this stage cannot be attained without any external help. The systemic mind is therefore no stranger to psycho-social support such as coaching, training, or therapy. With the ever-growing importance of the ideal of servitude, shame, till then a tenacious concomitant of accepting help ("You should be able to manage on your own; you must not make yourself dependent on other people's help"), fades into the background as a relic of personalistic consciousness.

From a systemic point of view, it is absurd for one person to judge another. Whenever we judge others we presuppose that there is a position from which one could judge another. Since every position is part of a system, judgment, too, is part of a system and can lay no claim to validity outside of it. Judgement born from the subjective view of a speaker is valid only within the system of this speaker. It makes little sense, then, even to voice a judgmental idea, as it can tell us nothing about the receiver, which it is intended to do.

In the face of perspective moral relativism at stage six, does every form of moral assessment become obsolete? May Hitler now set himself up alongside Gandhi and grin at the camera of history, applauded by the in-crowd of post-modernism?

Every stage of consciousness carries with it certain responsibilities of purifying and disinfecting itself and all previous stages. At every stage from 1 to 5, there are means to differentiate between good and evil and put criminals to justice: excommunication (1), Draconian measures (2), regulated court proceedings and standardized sentences (3), withdrawal of material goods (4), personal moral ostracism (5).

Down in the past and in less differentiated cultural circles, people have tended to confuse planes of consciousness. Thus, the divine power is asked to keep us from moral defilement by threatening gestures and thundering commands. Criminals should receive not only a worldly measure of punishment; they should be condemned for eternity by the will of God. God must be asked to preside over or assist in the regulation of social life so long as mortal arms are too weak to fight criminality. But as soon as the necessary worldly institutions function well enough to ensure peace and harmony within a community, God is no longer “harassed” with pleas for punishing moral offenders. People no longer demand of Him things that are not in His agenda. His plans are the essential object of study and experience at the seventh, the highest stage of consciousness.

At the sixth plane of consciousness, people know these mechanisms and often act as if they no longer had to concern themselves with them. What they are interested in is to increase their knowledge and understanding of things: they want to know what is actually happening when individuals or large organisations lose their control and do damage to their environment. Moral judgment, important though it is, will only be in the way of the learning process.

It is important that the moral dimension remains even though it has been relativized by systemic consciousness. Just as personalities are not done away with just because they lose their central importance, morality, too, is not given up simply because it is recognised as part of a broader context. However, moral issues are no longer discussed exclusively in terms of individual ideas. Misdeeds are recognised as misdeeds and are punished: they are not excused, even though the conditions under which they were done are also taken into consideration. Wrong is still wrong, and the blame is no longer exclusively on the wrongdoer.

To ensure this expansion of the framework of moral assessment as the basis for a balanced and functional social life, it takes some reinforcement of trust in people and institutions. Large and complex systems can only work if they are founded in trust, i.e. if I am taking a risk no one will take advantage of my momentary situation of exposure. In the economic sector, this mechanism has been tested and safeguarded to some extent. Every commercial transaction, including the monetary system since the introduction of paper money (as such, a worthless equivalent for value), is based on trust.

In tight communities, in which people directly depend on one another, there tends to be a greater amount of trust than in loosely knit structures, where many of the acquaintances are superficial and perfunctory (including of course virtual communities, where members can freely invent their identities).

In the wake of the formation of materialism and later the global community, the fear of the loss of reliability in relationships grows strong like never before. On an interpersonal level, trust can now no longer be based solely on personal reliability: it needs to be rooted in something deeper. People therefore need to explore the deep layers of their soul, where their unresolved fears lurk. Whenever a fear or trauma is resolved, another dimension of trust in the world we require to integrate in the complex web of the global community is liberated.

To practise the systemic plane of consciousness is to practise a new form of trust. At previous stages, the motto was, "Trust no one but yourself". If we abandon the idea that our own life is only about us, we will need to be able to trust the larger contexts we are part of.

Every system tends in some way towards perfection. It wants to use its own potential. To be able to do so, it requires a good relationship towards its environment. It remembers success- and harmful experiences, looking for new ways if the old ones prove ineffective. Often the majority of members of a system are ignorant of the ways how to develop it, which we will interpret as a problem. We will mistrust systemic consciousness, thinking that we must employ our individual idiosyncratic strategies to get on top of things. In retrospect, systemic wisdom has often proven superior to the isolated efforts of individuals. And this insight can serve as a great source of trust.

It takes a lot of time for trust to grow, and this process of growth can easily be disturbed: therefore, if we want to see this new form of consciousness to become a prevalent power in this world, we will probably have to be patient.

One of the factors that encourage trust in its growth is a new form of rationality that has been gaining influence in connection with the rise of systemic consciousness. This is characterised by a panoramic view of systems and their environment, suggesting the backing down of individual views and interests. As self-interested thinking ranks highly in the individual mind, the fears that make us hold on to it must be overcome. Only then will we be able to transcend our individual point of view and see not only the positions of other members of the system but the system as a whole and its environment.

Systemic reason involves the insight that what benefits the entire system also benefits its individual members, at least in the long run. To actually recognise this, we need to gain "systemic trust". Reason can enable us to forego smaller short-term profits for the sake of larger long-term profits.

The rationality of the systemic stage enables many people who have arrived at the limits of personalistic thinking to venture one step further. For this step to be taken, it is necessary to hold the Ego – to which the individual reality is restricted to the individual and the reality of the whole is only marginally accessible to the individual – at arm's length. The act of doing so could refer to a rational calculation: if I adopt this or that measure for the sake of the environment which will make my life more difficult in one way or the other, I may hope to contribute to improve the situation of the environment on the whole, which will sooner or later benefit me personally.

The step from the systemic to the final stage of consciousness represents an even greater challenge. We cannot pass the threshold to holistic consciousness unless we completely let go of the desire to increase our individual happiness. But if we manage to overcome our worst fears, we will gain access to an inner freedom that requires no promise of happiness because it throws open the doors to that for which we have ever yearned deep within our hearts.

A Farewell to Structures of Power and Violence

Systems with rigid structures of super- and subordination, whose golden thread is the notion of power, prove ponderous, inflexible and altogether not very productive. The powerful are eager to sustain and increase their power: all other purposes are subordinated to this one. How can the powers that be, then, ever make an essential contribution to the welfare of the entire system?

Systemic consciousness is therefore ready to fluidify such structures. Fixed positions with fixed opportunities of exerting power are replaced with functions adapted to the needs of the system rather than the desires of one of its elements. To systemic consciousness, one person in a certain position can basically be replaced with another, provided the latter has the required competences.

Systems aspire constantly to improve themselves by reducing the fears and thus encouraging the well-being of all its members. Power exerted for power's sake causes fear and must be curbed for systemic growth to happen.

A systemic point of view cannot be adopted unless the person attempting to adopt it willingly relinquishes power. That is the root of the idea of non-violence. By refusing to partake in the game of power, we enable ourselves to unmask its rules. When policemen hand down violence to people who refuse to defend themselves by choice, a higher power is revealed that is superior to violence. When we see images of monks being trampled down by the military apparatus, we feel compassion and anger. We sympathise with the systemic power of refusing to exert power, shocked to find that the strength of abstaining from violence is its weakness.

One bullet was enough to kill Mahatma Gandhi. For a short duration the stubborn, brutal power triumphs over higher wisdom. But the subtle power of the evolution of consciousness cannot be broken by violence. Deep down, people know that foregoing power is to pave the way for a better world. Though it may at times be risky not to participate in the game of power, some people will do so, thus contributing their share for the creation of ever more scope for freedom from power. Systemic consciousness is right behind this.

Violence is recognised as a dead end and as a mistake in interpersonal and international conflicts. Violence in the sense of exerting power by life-threatening means signifies the assertion of selfish interests by creating fear in other people. To create fear in other people is to take their freedom and to treat them with disrespect. Hence, the society should function without the exertion of violence. The monopolisation of violence, which was introduced by bureaucratic consciousness, finds itself under the surveillance of another control layer: a state exerting force must explain itself and will be held accountable if the violence has been found unjustified.

The prosecution of war criminality by international courts of justice, which was introduced shortly after world war two, was finally blessed with wider acceptance towards the end of the 20th century. However, for the instigation and non-prevention of war to be made into internationally punishable crimes, systemic consciousness will have to gain a larger following and to become yet more firmly established in people's moral understanding.

Violence is like an epidemic: its victims will themselves commit violent acts, becoming thus part of a great chain of destruction, whose outcome is disastrous. This sequence of violence and counter-violence, which is also one of accusation and counter-accusation (referred to as "punctuation" by Paul Watzlawick) may end where a systemic point of view can be adopted. It is from such a point of view that we can see with understanding the position of the enemy who has made us suffer. Thus, the ancient wisdom that walking in the moccasins of the enemy leads to peace re-enters history at a higher stage of consciousness.

The condemnation of violence now refers not only to physical force but is extended to all levels of communication; both emotional and verbal violence are decried. Mobbing, social exclusion and discrimination are all recognised as forms of violence. The exploration and disposal of the causes for people's willingness to use force become a central aim of a society looking for peace not only on an international level but also internally.

A particular focus of systemic consciousness is the resolution of conflicts with communicative methods rather than by violent means. Such communicative methods are especially devised to prevent that one of the warring factions lose face and long to take revenge in their humiliated state of mind. Conflicts can be resolved only if both parties learn to respect and be well-wishing towards the other.

The systemic approach is fragile and vulnerable. A single destructive act of violence can cause a well-planned peace process to fail. People and organisations tend to fall back on the more primitive means while they are not making real headway with the systemic methods. When the balancing powers of a system are not yet taking effect, what is required of us is faith and patience; but these qualities will be lost all too easily if we are still addicted to the speed and restlessness of previous stages.

These are, however, the only effective and lasting solutions. In the long run, steamrolling egos and berserk machines of violence can never win. History has shown this over and over again: it has a very long breath.

The walls of power have become brittle, and in different places they make room for new social experiments to happen. The foundation of these walls is the rigid hierarcho-bureaucratic structure, which supports row upon row of the grey, cold, uniform stone blocks of administration and optimisation carved by materialistic consciousness. At the worn margins of the edifice, however, are placed other architectural phenomena of personalistic and later systemic origin. These alternative models of organisation grow in the course of time, becoming proud, prominent complementary structures. These organisations call on the old system to clear away its crust of bureaucratic rigidity and to expand beyond its materialistic idea of man. They refer to the great weaknesses intrinsic to the system, enforcing a kind of transformation that involves the inclusion of the personalistic and systemic spirit. Examples for such alternative sectors of society can be found in complementary medicine, progressive education, wellness culture, organic farming, environmentally friendly means of transportation, as well as the humanisation of the economy.

The End of Fixations and Alternative Thinking

Many of these social, cultural and scientific paradigms, which followed World War Two, departed from some of the most fundamental ideas of modernity. Well into the twentieth century, history was widely held to follow a linear course, during which man steadily ascended to ever greater moral heights. In view of the ruins and scattered bodies, what was left of this optimism? Only question marks.

The absolutisation of interpretation and judgment came under heavy systematic criticism, which lasted until doubt, scepticism and personal disintegration gave way to the wisdom of the systemic interconnection of all phenomena. This opened the door for all of man's traditions and insights, welcome to appear on the same stage as harmonising equals. Out of this rich treasure, the creative designs of the age are made, appearing in all kinds of combination. Anything is possible and everything is allowed is the motto of post-modernism.

Life in groups prepared people for a subtle understanding of systems. However, it is only at this stage of evolution that we become aware of and are able to do away with the limitations of unconscious group processes. Groups tend to, for instance, ascribe fixed roles to their members – leading figure, power behind the throne, fellow traveller, jester, driving force, damper. The reason why this worked for so long is that role assignments lend a feeling of safety, keeping in check the fear of being ousted from the group. Group dynamics, however, inevitably lead to difficulties that cannot be surmounted by fixed role assignments. Some conflicts cannot be resolved by personalistic strategies. Personalistic consciousness tends to attribute fixed qualities to individuals, like tattoos: a person is this way or that, once and for all. Prejudices are formed and established, and the perspective of change is blocked. This dynamic can be escaped only if systemic consciousness is chosen as the starting point. Systemic consciousness refers to the experience of the present moment. All prejudices must be abandoned, so that a system may bring forth all it has at its disposal to solve problems.

Systemic thinking is more taxing and more time-consuming and requires great flexibility. It is a professional attitude that must be rehearsed and perfected. Our view of people is normally filtered through personalistic spectacles, which often render them unchangeable and immoveable save by the application of pressure. So we need to liberate our habitual patterns of perception and learn to see the bigger in the smaller and the smaller in the bigger.

Science has long been considering the question what is innate and what is learned. Findings in the field of genetic research have shown that genes do not simply run an automatic programme but are activated according to the requirements of the situation. This alternative then does not really make sense. Other either-or problems, such as the famous question whether light consists of particles or of waves, prove invalid.

Many dichotomies, then, are being exploded these days; the long-standing tradition of thinking in polarities is losing its power. Therefore, we may to abandon the illusory idea of an objective world that can be represented by figures. After all, this was merely a projection of materialistic consciousness in the interest of dominating nature.

According to chaos theory, we just cannot predict in most (and in the most relevant) cases when and how what changes will befall. At this stage, it is therefore possible to speak of miracles again, of the improbable and the surprising, as every now and then we will experience things we would not have expected to happen in the context they take place in. The most radical changes in human history as well as individual lives can and could not be predicted, including the paradigm shifts that lead from one stage of consciousness to the next.

The freedom of systemic thinking is revealed in the fact that the weight can easily be shifted from quantifiability to the immaterial quality of relation-ships. While relationships require material starting points, they themselves are not material. How Peter feels about Susan is something we cannot perceive with the senses used to represent material objects but with a "sixth" sense, i.e. the one which perceives on a systemic level.

Relationships know no measured or market values, but are experienced in unquantifiable qualities and in the finest nuances. A statement like „I appreciate you by 85 per cent", for instance, has a strange ring. If we concentrate on qualities, all ideas will lose their claim to absolute truth. Any assertion exists only in relation to the speaker – always and in principle.

The principle of networking thus shifts the attention from material objects to relationships. As no material object can assert a predominant role, all existing relations are considered equal. Therefore, nature is now no longer regarded as an object, neither of exploitation (materialism) nor of desire and admiration (personalism). It is revalued as subject, as interlocutor to man on many different levels.

There is therefore a renewed interest in the likes of shamans, miracle healers and psychics. They are no longer condemned as superstitious or fraudulent scum: they enjoy popularity in the roles of healers and interpreters of human life. It is they who know the channels of communication with the forces of nature, and they know how to use them. The intelligence of the Earth (*Gaia*) is respected and heard speaking in her own voice.

Systemic consciousness, then, is inherently ecological. All systems must entertain a poised relationship with their environment: without it, they would perish. Therefore, every system forms a meta-system with its environment, in which mutual concerns are negotiated. In a wider context, this is man's relationship with nature, which can no longer be seen merely in the light of human interest but whose needs must be respected just as much.

At the materialistic stage, environmentally friendly thinking is employed only where behaviour damaging to the environment produces higher costs than ecological measures will. Both ecological "gain" and "loss" must be expressible in figures to be of importance to the materialist.

Personalistic consciousness treasures the individuality of nature, its own personality. The Romantic love for mystifying nature deepens man's understanding of the importance of nature for his well-being. Nature is protected and supported as object of human desire and ideology.

Systemic consciousness enables us to think in the spirit of nature, as if we ourselves were nature. Our actions are determined by this. Equipped with mathematical data, scientific models and the sensitivity of a nature lover, we understand the workings of nature from within. Ideally, this perspective will then influence all political and economic decisions.

The Attitude of Serving

> Those who want to live long must serve; but those who want to dominate will not live long. (Hermann Hesse, Journey to the East)

One of the fears that must be conquered before it is possible to find a way out of the confines of personalistic consciousness and enter the systemic stage is the fear of meaninglessness. This is a precursor of the fear of losing the ego-consciousness. Whoever manages to overcome it is given the opportunity to assume an attitude of serving where the welfare of the system is more important than individual advantage.

What we are not referring to here are the kinds of servitude found at earlier stages of consciousness. We cannot, for instance, apply the terminology of master and slave that Hegel used, describing a relation of co-dependency between one who commands (and is forced to do so) and another who has no other choice but to obey.

Much rather, it is the idea of the free person, who in no way whatsoever has to answer to a system of rulership, that paves the way for the new form of servitude. First of all, the liberated individual wants to "run free" in whatever she has always been dreaming of, filling her spaces of freedom with the pursuit of her personal interests. Once the desires of the individual have been fulfilled and have lost their original appeal, the focus shifts to the neighbour and to the entire world.

The new attitude of serving is not a product of sheer necessity or conformity but of the self-confidence of the freeman who needs no slave to boost his ego. His connection to systemic consciousness, which provides a framework of orientation and support, is enough to motivate his service. A relinquishment of satisfying the ego that is not a product of self-denial or manipulative victim mentality but of the conquest of the fear of lack, leads to what we refer to as commitment: the employment of one's own physical and mental powers for a cause. Instead of exerting ourselves merely for our own sake, we will do so with a view of benefitting others or the world at large.

Selfless service can result in incredible achievements: people who in spite of adverse conditions help day and night like Doctors Without Borders, helping victims of war and natural disasters to their feet, fighting diseases or exerting themselves for the rights of minorities and the future of the planet.

To people as yet unable to comprehend the systemic stage of consciousness, any attitude of serving will appear as contemptible self-adulation or self-abasement. Therefore, it is often a target of ridicule. Instead of judging the mockers, however, we should first try to understand the fears, unconquered and thus impeding to progress, of which the mockery is a symptom.

Assuming an attitude of servitude is the beginning of a whole idea of personal doership. As our actions are no longer determined by strategic considerations as to personal advantage, the very goal or hoped for result of our actions fades into the background, while doership gains in instrinsic value. We see the goal of our action in action itself rather than regarding our performance as a means for any separate goal. The time structure is thus reduced to the present moment, to the here and now, and we find ourselves standing at the threshold to universalistic consciousness.

With this attitude we emancipate ourselves from the materialistic patterns of stress, laying down the burden of performance pressure. Our physical needs are again involved in the performative framework. The limits of human capacities are respected in the planning phase so that we may perform free from pressure and without exploiting ourselves internally. Among the preconditions for this form of motivation to show to advantage is a relatively stress-free working environment.

Communities

The lone-wolf mentality is replaced with team spirit. From the systemic point of view it becomes clear that all magnificent deeds attributed to one person actually required the support of many helping hands. At the systemic stage, the efficiency of team work is held more important than that of the individual performance.

"Caesar defeated the Gauls. Didn't he at least take a cook with him?" wondered Bert Brecht. It took decades for the general public to realise that the first ascent of Mount Everest was not in fact the individual achievement of a Western mountaineer but a joint achievement with a team and, on the last stretch, with a Nepalese Sherpa. What could be offensive to personalistic consciousness is a delight to systemic consciousness: to associate with the first ascent of Mount Everest (Sagarmatha or Chomolunga) not only Edmund Hillary but also Tensink Norgay – as a symbol for a global community that will reach the top by means of cooperation rather than antagonism.

Systemic consciousness falls back on tribal themes, using the potential of ancient human experience for the modern world. The formation of communities at the systemic stage is not based on origin: it is no longer the blood that connects their members but a common orientation, a common cause. Membership to a modern "tribe" is not a lifelong engagement, nor is it enforced by hierarchical rules. Much rather, it depends on the goals and purposes people have set themselves by free choice. By these new communities, however, needs are satisfied that people have long suffered for lack of fulfilment – in fact, ever since they were driven out of the "paradisiacal" safety zone of their ancient tribes.

New tribes are like nets which are wide-meshed but may offer enough safety to cushion the loss involved in the abandonment of the personalistic life philosophy. Also, they may help ensure that pathological developments are no longer linked to individual people to be then passed on to institutions for their administration, but feathered by way of referring to the needs underlying them.

Arts and Entertainment

Art has a crucial role to play as initiator of this stage of consciousness. By the beginning of the 20th century, art had in many places dropped its role of prettifying and colouring the dull routine of a materialistic wasteland, and equally that of attacking society for its alienation in the name of personalistic rebellion. New forms of expression evolved that could no longer be contained within the limits of materialistic or personalistic consciousness.

In visual art, the spread of abstract art marked the beginnings of a deconstruction of the basic concept of objective perspectives. The door was then open for a whole new way of perceiving the world. At around the same time, atonal and twelve-tone music pointed out the same direction. It was no longer oriented at bourgeois consumer habits or the organic realities of hearing but obeyed abstract construction principles which ignored the expectations of the general public.

The more systemic consciousness enters the mainstream of the cultural climate, the more the role of art in the vanguard of consciousness diminishes. While it continues to support the process of the spreading of systemic approaches by the creativity of its productions, other channels of communication now come to the fore that are more apt to represent the aspect of relations. The production of art is closely connected with the individuality of the artist, in which respect it will always be tied to personalistic consciousness. At the systemic stage, however, the great masterminds fade into the background. The creative potential of art becomes one dynamic component among many equal powers working for the release of social and cultural tensions.

As around the world the walls tumble down in the systemic context, all artistic traditions in the world rise in global esteem. Communicative connection leads to links and overlaps between all kinds of artistic production, without the strict separation of high and popular culture, mainstream and alternative art, classicism, modernism or post-modernism. Minority and underground culture is regarded with interest, and local traditions are revalued.

People strive to create a dynamic balance between performance and relaxation. The mechanisms of stress and physical emaciation are revealed, and people consciously countersteer them. They engage in sporting activities, striving for fitness and wellness. This form of consciousness knows no polarities; the systemic approach is therefore always aimed at integrating relaxation and performance, i.e. excluding harmful and chronic stress from the dynamics of performance. This is sometimes successful if performance is linked with entertainment so that productive activities take place in a relaxed atmosphere. Entertainment is introduced into the context of production instead of serving as a focal point of escapism in a cruel, exploitative world (fun society).

The danger that new patterns of addiction might become attached to the desire for entertainment and its satisfaction must be realised and defused. The only way this may take effect is if discipline is internalised, that is if it becomes a factor of enjoyment in its own right. The missing link between the classical antipodes of effort and leisure is the aforementioned idea of servitude. Individual achievement is dedicated to the realisation of something, and if this grows, every activity performed in the intention of serving it will be a feast of joy. The organic principle, according to which growth is happiness, is regained in the attitude of servitude. Just as every organelle serves the overall purpose of the cell and will probably feel joy if things are running smoothly, so can we acknowledge the ways in which our actions benefit something higher and feel happy if it grows. At this stage, all work is ultimately done in the interest of a universalistic global community – it is just that some activities contribute more indirectly than others to this end.

The luxury of the systemic stage is neither in the consumption of goods nor solely in the consumption of the extraordinary and the extravagant (as in personalistic consciousness) but in a factor of enjoyment that is in a completely new way linked to discipline. The body and its signals are recognised as valid correctives. Systemic man is physically aware. The enjoyment of the activity in itself, regardless of the belated satisfaction it promises, is the motor of activity.

Love and Relationships at the Systemic Stage

With all the uncertainty and brittleness that man-woman relationships are subject to at the personalistic stage, new points of view are required, which systemic thinking can provide. The two main questions concerning love at the personalistic stage are how to maximise it and what method to employ to generate it: "How does one manage to love truly?" (Alexandre Jardin). This concept of love, then, is still oriented at the materialistic principles of feasibility and quantifiability, representing therefore one of the productive misdirections on the quest for the philosophers' stone of love.

The systemic point of view is one step further removed from materialism. The question of systemic consciousness is: under what circumstances can love grow, and how can we create them? The individual asks herself how she can contribute to the success of the relationship, i.e. what she can do to make the other person in the relationship happy and secure.

There is a change of direction, from taking to giving – but not in a naively selfless way. Only by giving in the right way will we eventually get what we need: therefore we give. We give trusting that this will benefit the relationship, and that in due time whatever we need will be returned.

Personalistic consciousness was still dominated by the fear of not getting enough – a consequence of the personal isolation and emotional strain in capitalism, but also a heritage of earlier days, where fear of lack often meant fear of starvation. The basic structure remains the same but the object of fear is transferred from the material to the emotional sphere, there losing itself in randomness. Emotions are, after all, flighty and ever-changing. How can we, then, ever be sure what is too little, enough, or too much? How can I differentiate between what I should change in order to get what I need, and what the other person should change so that I may get enough.

In systemic consciousness, insatiable emotions are removed from the centre, being, however, assigned an appropriate place nearby. They must be respected, as they would otherwise develop a destructive potential. They can, however, no longer set the tone and establish the guiding principles for action. Systemic reason appears as a playmate, not as a ruler of the emotional landscapes.

All the elements important to the people involved should be recognised and appreciated as to their significance. The system will not be in a balanced state before all elements have reached a satisfactory degree of contentment. Therefore it is important for everyone to make an effort until such a state has been attained.

Our concept of love thus turns from an ostensibly measurable quantity into a functional term referring to the ideal balance in a dynamic system. In this way, systemic thinking allows love to "flow" and to "float". It reveals that love is ever-present in the web of existence, and the human form of love is just one aspect of it. Love can be likened to the force of attraction between a nucleus and its electrons, to centrifugal and centripetal force, which determine the course of the heavenly bodies, and to a successful form of communication between two single-celled organisms.

With this extension, love breaks free from the net of flighty emotion in which it was caught by romance ("love comes and goes"). The romantic is helplessly exposed to the swells of love – if it comes he is on cloud nine, if it goes he is deeply despaired. Love to him is an unpredictable power he is at the mercy of.

The perspective of systemic consciousness is consoling and disillusioning at the same time: love is not a feeling, and, rather than coming and going, it is a constant, powerful presence. What does come and go is our personal relationship with it: as soon as we find ourselves in the grip of fear, we will fail to recognise love or make room for it. Then we will cease to feel loved and will experience other people as loveless.

That is the reason why we took to classifying love as a feeling in the first place: when the fear is gone, we can love again – consequently, love must be a feeling just like fear. What really happens is that in the grip of fear we see only ourselves and the danger we are exposed to. As soon as this egocentric fixation is overcome, we again find ourselves connected with others, experiencing this liberation and contact as a feeling. In reality, as soon as the fear began to fade away, we opened up to something that had been there all along – powerful, supportive, and connecting.

Love, then, is a lot more than just an emotion, although its human form makes use of various feelings to take effect. It does not make use of the demoniac forces associated with it at the personalistic stage, instead aspiring to universalistic grandeur. The systemic concept of love becomes the gateway to holistic consciousness.

What this means for relationships is that a deeper understanding of the partner's otherness can be a source of trust in him. The clearance of dogmatism and egotism in relationships makes room for devotion to the wonderful aspects of every encounter. Consciousness transcends the limits of the individual and embraces the other. People learn to trust the system and its power to set wrongs to right.

If there are conflicts, they can no longer be ended by exerting power and implementing unilateral interests. The focus shifts from the people involved to their relationship. The aim is no longer to find out who did what wrong and should change. The main object of reflection is not individual responsibility but the relationship. What was it about the relationship that caused the conflict? Instead of vying for power, people try to work out in conversation what the misunderstanding was.

The systemic motto is that everyone is always right, from her individual point of view. People try to achieve the best they are capable of achieving at any given moment. Accordingly, it will appear pointless to search out the wrongdoer in the relationship and condemn his or her behaviour. The only chore left to do is then to purify the relationship, i.e. to clear away what inhibits the flow of communication.

Establishing love, or much rather re-attaining the state of love, is then neither a secret nor a task requiring extensive learning or a lot of practice. It is to identify and overcome whatever impedes understanding.

Religion and the Sacred

At the systemic stage, every religion has a place, but no religion comes first. Rather, by comparing the diverse religious traditions, we become aware that they all share a yearning for the same essential centre. In this core, there is no disagreement, and there are no contradictions. In the forecourt to salvation, however, minds lock horns. What images, if any, may we have of the centre, what words and what language should we use to describe it? Which aspect of the centre is the most important?

This is the place where endless debates take place: is Jesus identical in nature with God, the Heavenly Father? Did God appoint a representative on Earth, capable of formulating infallible theorems? Do souls pass from one life to the next, or are they brought before a last judgement after death?

At the systemic stage, the representatives of religious communities come to realise that they cannot spread their beliefs by violent means. They begin to concentrate their efforts on learning to understand the traditions of other creeds and denominations. In direct conversation, they often come to realise that although their paths may be different, the goal of their quest is the same.

Systemic consciousness paves the way for the holistic stage also in that the sacred is integrated into the profane. From this point of view, Jesus' miracles can be understood as indicating that the sacred and awe-inspiring is in fact part of our everyday existence – and that we can encounter it if we only abandon our limited perspectives.

The sacred is none other than the successful functioning of the universal. The individual need only open up to this perspective in order to realise that there is really no difference between here and the beyond, but that the two are intertwined with each other. The systemic revelation is that the two perspectives – of seeing life as profane or sacred – are equal and form a coherent whole. Spiritual peak states are accessible to every human being; the sacred is not reserved for extraordinary people with exquisite capabilities or uncommon religious diligence.

The treasure at the centre, which every religion seeks to find, is holistic consciousness. It transcends all speech communities and traditions, without denying any of them. It is free from power, because it owns and bestows all power. However, it does not use this vast resource of power to derogate or condemn religious orientations, practices, or positions. Instead, it remains faithful to the idea that is conceived already at the systemic stage: every religious community has an essential role to fulfil, lending people support and giving them orientation far beyond the trivial challenges of life. To cope with the unpredictabilities of life and with fate and mortality we require meaning-making concepts and procedures, which religions have offered for thousands of years.

Certain exponents of Enlightenment at the personalistic stage have tried to condemn religion lock, stock and barrel, and totalitarian systems have attempted to eradicate them. This will not benefit the evolution of consciousness. Religions will be there as long as people need them.

The Ambivalence of Systemic Consciousness

Systemic consciousness has no internal centre. Its free-flowing nature makes it liable to ambivalent developments. The dissolution of binding value systems tempts one to orient himself at the pragmatics of relative success. Newly developed psychological techniques, for instance, can be applied likewise for the benefit of other people and for the maximisation of private gain, even at the expense of others.

People still deeply rooted in materialistic and personalistic consciousness and determined by the fears from those stages tend to use systemic knowledge for their own purposes. Systemic consciousness possesses too few resources for self-purification to do well in countersteering this tendency. Via a clever utilisation of constructivist argumentation techniques, for instance, any questioning statement can be reflected back on the context of the questioner. "You think it's a shame if I use this technology for my own ends and to the disadvantage of others? How can you be sure if your ethic, too, doesn't benefit only yourself and hurt others like me?"

Inevitably, systemic consciousness tends towards randomness and relativism. Systemic constellations and entanglements are often infinite in principle and unmanageable. They can therefore not be restricted or controlled from within without contradicting their own principles.

Therefore, the evolution of consciousness must look for another stage, one that transfers the focus back to the inside, though it is this time a spectrum of the inside that encompasses not only the individual, the delimitative person itself.

The transition from stage six to stage seven is, quite understandably, a very difficult one: the task, after all, is to radically challenge the basic assumptions of systemic consciousness. There are, however, strong motives that drive the spirit of evolution on.

At stage six, doubt and scepticism are of great importance. They are a part of systemic rationality. Every model with a claim to truth must be examined and challenged by all means available. Thus, the wheat can be separated from the chaff. Naive or fraudulent promises of salvation, egotistic manipulations and short-sighted ideologies should be exposed and disempowered.

The seventh stage comes with the premise that man can in fact shed all his fears and thus gain access to his complete potential of understanding and creativity. At the systemic stage, this idea is received with scepticism. It can never be embraced there, as the fears characteristic to systemic consciousness are in the way of this, especially the fear of giving up the freedom inherent in diversity and relativity. Therefore, holistic consciousness is often banished to the dark corners of charlatanism, together with esoteric, neo-tribal, hierarcho-religious or pre-scientific suggestions for global salvation.

On the other hand, there is often a longing to be felt at the fringes of the systemic universe for completeness and eternal freedom. It becomes clear that many forms of individual and collective suffering can never be cured by the means that this stage of consciousness has to offer. And so long as the cure is not complete, consciousness pushes onward, seeking for new sources of strength and wisdom that systemic consciousness cannot even perceive.

Some of the "final" questions (such as, What is the root of evil? or What is man's true destiny?) are asked only by the restless mind. At stage six it comes up against a boundary it finds impossible to penetrate. Here it realises that all it can offer as an answer to the fundamental questions is models of relative validity. It can no longer lay claim to any objective truth. But this idea is not satisfactory to the mind.

The systemic mind holds that beyond every border there is a new land of revelation: but this, too, does not stretch on to infinity. The result would be an ever-expanding chain of metatheories. But when on realising the immeasurable richness of the moment, of the here and now, we stop asking questions, our mind will come to rest.

Systemic consciousness is a necessary preliminary stage for holistic consciousness. The concrete experience of concrete systems leads out of the confines of the ego's perspective of personalistic consciousness and paves the way for the more abstract forms of holistic experience. Already at the systemic stage we begin to see that an energy field transcending the limitations of the ego influences and directs our existence. As this wisdom can be expressed in the language of reason, ways of thinking are cultivated that enable us to ground the concept of holistic consciousness in experience. With its characteristic rationality, then, systemic consciousness provides the clarity it takes to connect the spiritual dimension of consciousness with other realities. Without this foundation, holistic consciousness would appear as a crumbling building of hollow phrases. However, without ascending to the next sphere of consciousness the human perspective will remain hopeless and absurd.

Our Inner Imprints of the Systemic Stage

At the threshold to adult maturity, we realise how complex the world really is. Self-centred ideas about their improvement are not enough, and the pursuit of isolated purposes is seen in a critical light. We begin to concern ourselves with the problems of social life, looking for ways of sorting them out.

Living in the modern world demands a great deal of flexibility and openness. The identity formed by personalistic consciousness in puberty must be relativized by the adult. It becomes clear that society distributes roles that everyone who wants to play along needs to accept. The exemption from rigid judgmentalism requires the development of well-reflected personal strength. As ideologies lose much of their credibility, the pragmatic attitude should be accompanied with inner integrity.

The rigorous ethic of personalistic consciousness is also taken back, as there are so many points of view and motives to consider. On the other hand, our appreciation of and commitment for many traditions, fringe groups and the preservation of nature increases.

How can we identify our own basic experiences of the sixth phase of the evolution of consciousness? Let us consider the fears, fixations and resources that can be attributed to this stage.

Characteristic Fears:

- Loss of personal profile
- Fear of overtaxation
- Fear of systemic complexity
- Fear of unwieldiness

Negative Fixations:

- Attachment to one's own identity and one's acquired characteristics, to subtle value judgments and justifications (the anxious egotist)

- Relativism, floating in randomness (the intellectual cynic)
- Over-emphasis of rationality, repression of emotions (the narrow-minded cerebral person)
- Employment of systemic knowledge for materialistic or personalistic purposes (the clever, flexible marketing person)

Resources:

- Freedom from all forms of condemnation
- Flexibility in thought and action
- The skill of distancing oneself from dysfunctional emotions
- Trust in universal contexts
- Solution-oriented points of view
- Interest in the hidden and the overlooked

Exercises

Systemic Perception

purpose: creating an internal image of a system

indication: feelings of disconnectedness from one's own family members

Instructions: Close your eyes and imagine the members of your family. Where in an imagined space would you locate your father and your mother? Where would you locate the other members of your family? Where would you locate yourself? How do you feel in your position?

What is the quality of your relationship to any one of those persons at the moment? What changes if you imagine this person to move further away from you or to come closer?

In this fashion, go through all the relationships and explore them.

How do you feel now, in your position? Has anything changed since you started the exercise?

Thus visualising your family internally can help clarify your position and point out any problem or error of communication.

Assumed Values and Attitudes

purpose: identifying and examining assumed values and attitudes

indication: inclinations towards prejudice and generalisation, recurring communication problems

Instructions: Think about the relationship of your parents. What values and attitudes were decisive for it? What about the relationships of your grandparents – on your mother's side, on your father's side or both? If your knowledge / power of imagination reaches even further back: what was your great-grandparents' relationship like?

Compare these relationships to the love relationships you have had in your life. What has changed? Considering all that you have read about systemic consciousness: do you think that the influence of this form of consciousness on your relationships has increased? If yes, how did you find out?

Conflict

purpose: clearing conflicts of the theme of guilt

indication: tendencies towards accusation at times of conflict

Instructions: Think of a conflict you were involved in recently. Now imagine that the conflict is really nobody's fault: what changes do you notice within? What will change if you assume that everyone involved did the best she could at the time?

Work and Servitude

purpose: clearing the idea of servitude from old concepts and redefining it

indication: suffering from the idea of being compelled to work

Instructions: What kind of work do you do to earn money? What do you experience as strenuous? What will change if you assume that with this work you are doing a service to others?

Is it a good kind of change? If not, what makes it so difficult to regard your work as a service? Is there anything you can change about your point of view to make it easier?

* * *

If you buy into the systemic point of view, you will gain a broadened horizon, which may avail you in all aspects of your life. You will no longer need to see yourself as the centre of the universe, although you will not have to defer your wishes and cravings. You will have the opportunity to change your communicative behaviour and learn to understand other people better.

Stage 7: Holistic Consciousness – On the Path to Perfection

The noble man is always at ease with himself. The inferior man is always anxious.

(Confucius)

The soft overcomes the hard; the weak overcomes the strong. There is no one in the world but knows this truth, and no one who can put it into practice.

(Lao Tzu)

Where paradoxon lights up, the system expires and life prevails.

(Emile Michel Cioran)

Key aspects:
completeness, timelessness, universality, inner freedom, and connection in love

Towards the end of her morning meditation, Clara contemplated the day that was about to begin. And as she did so, she felt gratitude for all the opportunities that life had opened up to her. First she would visit John, an old friend, who lay dying in a hospice. He had asked for a couple of songs, which she would sing to him. The last time she had been with him, she had said good-bye with both sadness and happiness in her heart: what had made her happy was the dignity and cheerfulness that John expressed despite the pain from which he suffered.

Then she would offer her services in looking after asylum seekers at the airport. Even though it was not easy to be confronted with all those fates while only having little help to offer, she was looking forward to seeing the people, who arrived with such trust and hope and who it was her job to carefully familiarise with the legal conditions in this country.

Shortly past mid-day, she had an appointment with the minister. She would be addressing a few serious points, and she appreciated his open ear and his sincerity. She knew that not everything she considered to be right was enforceable, but she also knew that faith, persistence and inner conviction led to the goal.

Soon afterwards, at the working conference, important decisions would have to be made. She was delighted that some new sponsors had been found for important projects and felt the drive and the creative enthusiasm that spurred her and the others in the group on.

Later she would meet up with a friend to talk about the article she had promised her for a magazine. There would be enough time to talk about so many things dear to their hearts. Maybe they would take a walk, thus enjoying the evening in nature.

It was easy for her to mentally immerse all the events that were to take place today in a powerful, bright light. Her heart grew warmer as she thought of the many people she was to meet today, including those who would rush by her on the street and in the subway. What a gift this life was!

Liberation from Fear

Holistic consciousness recognises the connectedness of everything that exists, and the equal value of each element and each relation. Each element radiates with individual beauty. Universal connectedness is regarded as the true form of love.

Holistic consciousness is one important step ahead of systemic consciousness. Systems are stuck with their inert evolutionary inclinations. They can never fully understand these inclinations, and they will always try to wield a considerable influence on the development of other systems. It may be possible to introduce external stabilizers and control layers, which can, for example, monitor the correct use of means and step in if something is getting out of hand. But every system will remain liable to break down, as the internal systems of its members (and their individual fears) may run counter to the rules of the overall system. For instance, the employee of a charitable organisation, driven by an inner fear and resulting greed, may embezzle moneys in such clever ways that the damage will long remain undiscovered.

No system can have complete control over the individuals that belong to it. Subjective desires and motivations are not subject to laws or predictability. Therefore, interpersonal control is restricted to the perceivable aspects of human behaviour.

It is probably for the best that in spite of their considerable progress in the area of the observation of brain activities, neuroscience is still light years away from the possibility of depicting the inner processes involved in thinking and feeling. Imagine a society where all people have to run around with computerized tomography scanners on their heads ...

Dystopian models of a fully monitored society, such as 1984 or Fahrenheit 451 show that even in the densest net of monitoring the individual will still look for gaps and loopholes. The inexhaustible, basically infinite complexity of the human psyche is far more sophisticated than any system of observation devised by man.

There will always be individuals who will question the integrity of established systems. Where can we find the perfect social system? Which is the ideal educational system? Which form of economy guarantees the greatest success? They realise that systems always follow only certain interests and cannot act on behalf of the whole, as they have basically no access to it. In systemic consciousness, after all, there can be no Archimedean point from which the total of all systems could be viewed.

Therefore, no system can prevent the infection of internal individual action by selfish interests. Should, for instance, an educational system cater to the interests of the economy, those of the state, those of their individual consumers, or those of the pupils and students? And if it does follow the interests of the economy, should the training be oriented at a traditional or a progressive form of economy? Representatives of one sector try to shape the system according to their own interest, representatives of the other do the same.

How far such infections can spread shows how strongly people are still driven by their fears. The latter become subtler and subtler the further systemic consciousness develops. Who would suspect a hidden fear behind the lobbyists' endeavours to follow their interests within a political system. However, the subtler the fear becomes, the more egomaniacal a system can grow. Which financial services provider with his clever stockbrokers juggling the billions, is really aware of the fears that cause greed and megalomania in his system? Therefore, the evolution of consciousness cannot stop at the level of systemic models: it must venture the leap onto the next level, at which, in a wholly new manner, inner worlds seek harmony with the systems of external reality.

The Path to Inner Freedom

Entering holistic consciousness is possible only if the fears are dissolved. Through all ages and stages of consciousness, fear has been the power behind the throne. Fear has unleashed wars, oppressed people, and spurred the ransacking of the planet. Each new stage of consciousness promises to overcome fear. However, all stages previous have caused new problems and thus new fears. The promise of capitalism, for instance, was to check the fears of starvation and being killed by frost. While in some places of the world this has been successfully done, none of the rich countries have actually eradicated poverty, and the wealthy suffer from their own fears.

Fear enforces progress but prevents the optimal employment of reason and creativity. Therefore, the overcoming of boundaries does not bring true freedom if it is motivated by fear. Fears have to be directly confronted and dissolved to such an extent as to ensure that they do not influence important planning procedures, decisions, or actions. Then we can create a society informed by peace and justice.

How should we, then, go about exorcising our fears? In the chapter on organic preconditions, we said that fears result from the protective state of the organism. As we have seen, entire communities and cultures may develop collective fears and mobilise corresponding protective mechanisms. Dangers are internalised once they have been experienced: they are saved lastingly and are re-experienced in similar situations, no matter if those situations involve real dangers or not. In such situations, we easily forget to apply an appropriate reality check, as individuals or as whole societies.

We know from psychotherapy, and in particular from trauma therapy, that fear can be overcome only if the original situation is relived in a safe environment and integrated into the growth state. Also, it is now known that original traumatic situations can date far back in our personal history and are therefore buried deep in the subconscious. And we may now presume that a great number of these traumatisations happened prior to our birth and that the history of our fear memory reaches even beyond conception.

The exploration of our individual history of fear goes hand in glove with the development of methods and techniques to overcome our fears. Today, we are therefore able to sort out our personal fears and the disorders resulting from them. Decoupled from the reaction of fear, similar situations will then no longer trigger fear. If a fear has been exorcised, productive and cooperative action may take its place. Communication, reconcialition and peace will blossom in this new realm of inner freedom.

On the individual level there is then no other path to holistic consciousness than that of processing fear in therapy. Additional support is provided by traditions of meditation and meditative practices, mostly from Asia, which open the door to a fearless perception of the present moment, thus representing an effective means for finding serenity and inner freedom. Less afraid parents bring up less afraid children; less afraid teachers have less afraid pupils. Such circles are a necessary element of the path to liberation.

For progress to happen on a socio-political level, therapeutic and meditative work alone will not be enough. As long as the existing structures of power load the majority of people with enormous burdens so that they have to ensure their own survival, certain real fears will still be perpetuated. Societies whose members are able to ensure their own survival on a comfortable basis and moreover make enough surplus have the responsibility and the duty to join in the fight of the continuously produced fears. Even in the more developed societies, fear will not decrease before peace and justice rule the world. For it is the fears incorporated by the people and structures of the wealthy countries that greatly impede progress in less developed societies.

Therefore, it is in the interest of every society and every one of its members to contribute to the establishment of peace and justice. No cultural region, no state can long sustain peace and affluence when misery, hunger, and inequality are all around. What will disappear at the final stage of the evolution of consciousness is the fear that favours the attachment to personal advantage before the virtue of sharing and the orientation at personal profit before an attitude of servitude. With the passing of the fear of losing privileges, every reason will dematerialise for withholding from the world whatever we can contribute to make it a better place.

But how can societies get rid of their collective fears? The analogue to the individual therapeutic processing of traumatic wounds is the work of historical studies on the collective level. The exact knowledge and unbiased view of the shocking experiences a culture had in the course of its history will shed light on the collective fears from which people suffer and which are frequently instrumentalised by politicians to increase their power. The latter should be opposed by a public discourse that brings social scientific findings to the consciousness of the masses. Historical enlightenment reconciles us with the fate of our own collective, helping us to perceive the tasks of present and future without any ideological distortions.

The Great Interwovenness

Holistic consciousness turns up in places where all tendencies to pursue individual interests have been overcome. Particularity and individualism are not overcome by force or need. It happens to the measure in which people experience that they have been dwelling in a world of illusionary needs and imaginary fears and could feel better if they oriented themselves instead at the universal good.

The whole remains in the foreground, no matter what happens. The system of systems itself is no longer a system: the abstract distance required for viewing a larger context as a system is overcome by a more direct and concrete experience of the whole as a flow, as an ever-changing tapestry. The image of weaving (and being woven) may illustrate how in this world view the material and the immaterial come together.

The world as a woven structure of ever-changing forms is beyond the possibilities of scientific or artistic models. At the borders of the explainable, there is, however, room for wonder and simplicity. Consciousness remembers its own mythical origins, yet the naivety of holistic consciousness has been bathed in and cleansed by the holy waters of all the stages of consciousness. The essential aspects of stage one in particular are revalued and made accessible in a new form to a modern society.

To the holistic mode of thinking, the constructivist point of view is insufficient. Behind all the relative insights and reconstructions in models, there is *one* truth. This truth is based on the experience of the mystical as opposite pole to the material world. It is a realm beyond the reach of an unambiguous language, the realm of the paradoxical and the multi-layered. This is why Wittgenstein said that we can only be silent about it. However, all that can be said about it is said and should even be said, although it is clear that what is meant is infinitely more than what is said. Holistic discourse, then, feels its way towards the divine, and holistic consciousness gets closest to it.

The many realities, which at the systemic stage appear as parallel truths in the spirit of tolerance and respect, lead out of narrow-mindedness and pave the way for a global community. The post-modern randomness which results from this development is, however, not the last word. Beyond the mental constructions of insights tied to their contexts, holistic consciousness registers a powerful reality by which everything is brought forth, all the constructions of systemic consciousness included.

For the last turn human consciousness can take, a long leap of faith is required. Not the individual will, not the orientation chosen by a system determines the way things go, but a force behind these, a power that is subject to no other power, incomprehensible and enigmatic to the human mind. What we can recognise is the general direction, the evolution of consciousness, as it is modelled here.

We know how difficult it can be to get involved with the force behind all earthly things and to entrust oneself with it. For if we have to admit that we are not in fact the authors of the play of life but characters directed by a higher power, we will be denuded of our opportunities to take our destiny into our own hands. We will have no other option but to accept whatever happens to or around us, including the things we do or do not do.

Holistic experiences can be found in the context of any stage of consciousness. However, if these experiences are not embedded in a broader social context, they may easily be misunderstood and misapplied. Spiritual awakening is frequently connected with the experience of special personal powers used to exorcise old fears.

Such peak experiences all too easily combine with a lust for power still governed by subconscious fears. Then, the holistic experience itself becomes the tool of an earlier plane of consciousness. The epics are full of tales about the entanglement of spiritual with worldly power. The dramas from these stories provide for the themes of the *Nibelungenlied* (*The Song of the Nibelungs*) as well as of *The Lord of Rings*.

Only at the stage of holistic consciousness is it possible to effectively separate the wheat from the chaff. True liberty is to be free not only from the chains other people put on one but from the desire for power, from self-tyranny, vice and egotism.

At this stage we command a discriminative power which enables us to distinguish between that which grows from fear and that which grows from love. The actions motivated by love alone stand the test. Only they will have an all-round beneficial effect on society.

Purifying Spirituality

All the teachings and promises in the esoteric field are brought before this critical trial. All the early forms of spirituality must be revised where they fail to benefit the human soul; all universal and particular promises of salvation have to stand the test. The stronger the beacon of holistic consciousness shines, the greater is the responsibility of its followers and the mouthpieces of spirituality to lead a good life of integrity.

Such tests, however, will not be inquisition-like trials; the aim is not to defend a certain teaching but to pave the way for certain inner qualities. The individual himself is called upon to account for his own inner qualities. The greater the influence of holistic consciousness on society, the higher the demand on people for reflecting on their motives and admitting to their shortcomings. Where traces of fear are left to interfere, the halo is brittle.

There are more and more people whose consciousness and skill for this kind of discrimination increase. People then believe neither the pied pipers of spirituality, nor the self-elected saviours, nor the obscure occultist theories about the world and his wife, nor the prophecies from coffee grounds or from the scriptures of hierarchical consciousness, nor the systems of conspiracy-related paranoia; nor will they down these esoteric mixed drinks from jumbled-together tribal and post-tribal religious elements. All these figures, theories, and promises will sooner or later leave the market of ideologies of bliss.

Yet the sceptics of personalistic and systemic consciousness fight this position that seems to ignore the law of relativity. Whoever talks of holistic consciousness is therefore quickly accused of idealism. It is very easy to put the seventh stage down as a fairy-tale, as wishful fantasy. The holistic dimension of reality is no "hard" fact – it is revealed only when we are in a certain state of mind. For a great part of these phenomena we have some kind of explanation, others simply leave us dumbstruck.

To the sceptic, one look at the history of mankind is enough to conclude that a just society built on humanitarian principles can never exist. History as "slaughter bench" mankind (Hegel) cannot be denied, and man, "carved of such crooked wood that he can never be straight" (Kant), will always be fallible and seducible in the sceptic's view.

It is not sufficient to refute these sceptical antitheses to holistic optimism by referring to the limited nature of the stages of consciousness from which they originate. Perhaps the only hope of establishing that holistic consciousness is relevant is by simply pointing out its existence. So long as it is no recognised factor within the community, so long as it cannot fall back on experiences that are widespread and communicated on a broader basis, so long as it cannot claim conspicuous successes and victory marches in the formation of public opinions, it is vulnerable and easily attacked. Through the ages, representatives of holistic consciousness have often been accused of blind idealism and practical incompetence. In the perspective of the other stages of consciousness, the weapons and arguments holistic consciousness can use to defend itself are ridiculously feeble. In the first round, as it were, the brutal and tough always triumphs over the gentle and soft.

In trying to implement holistic consciousness, then, we seem at first to enter unsafe territory. We assume here that the realisation of a new stage of consciousness follows from the inner logic of evolution, which has a great impact on the course of history. If problems cannot be solved on one plane of consciousness, the formation of new organisation principles is called for. This dynamic allows systemic consciousness to raise itself above its station.

It is therefore not merely wishful thinking, the imaginings of a perfect world as a comfort amidst suffering. It is the power of progressive creativity, which motivates people to fight social evils and negative developments. And for this power to take full effect and not remain caught in fruitless circles, a new quality of thinking and acting is required.

Of course, our task of portraying a society governed by holistic consciousness must involve a great deal more speculation than that of depicting any other kind of society. After all, up to now this stage has been reached only on the individual level. It has never manifested in a larger social structure. We have no historical data to draw upon to say anything about the impact holistic consciousness would have on a collective level if a sufficiently large number of people had reached this stage. We can, therefore, only speculate about what it would bring with it for an entire society or for mankind in general if this stage of consciousness were the dominant factor of influence on them.

Modern consciousness was formed by Enlightenment, which has weakened the influence of religion on the general public and reduced the religious practice to a wholly private matter. Since then, every new model of society referring to religious issues has been eyed with scepticism; holistic consciousness itself has not been spared this kind of treatment.

We need to clarify that religion and spirituality are not absolutely synonymous. Religion is here defined as a certain form of spirituality. This form includes worldly structures, such as church hierarchies and fixed rituals and belief systems. By spirituality, on the other hand, we mean man's relationship to the whole, which is beyond sensory perception. In the course of history, religion has played a significant part in the development and propagation of spirituality. They have brought forth important spiritual teachers and have attempted to integrate the spiritual practices into the everyday routine of society.

On the other hand, with their worldly responsibilities, all religions have arranged themselves in one way or the other with the prevalent systems of power. In doing so, they in some ways compromised their spiritual ideology. Since the late Middle Ages and the days of Enlightenment, the resulting contradictions have been vehemently criticised in occidental Christianity and, with the victory march of materialistic consciousness, linked with the condemnation of spirituality in general. Consequently, as we have pointed out, a pragmatic form of atheism was embraced in wide circles of modernised society.

Spirituality, which is the basis of holistic consciousness, is not tied to any religion in particular. This allows for greater independence from the structures of power and dogmatic teachings. This kind of spirituality refers to experiences that people live through inwardly, while in contact with nature or through their interaction with other people. It requires no set form, no ritual, no sacred place. The spirit of God "breathes where it pleases". We can experience this spirituality wherever we are, provided we open up towards it. It will be there for us if we only venture beyond our limited perspectives and delusions.

The scorn of Enlightenment regarding religion was directed not against what liberated people or reconciled them with the natural hardships of life, but against the manipulations by which the trust of the people was abused for vile purposes in the name of God. A free spirituality founded in authentic experiences can be denied only by those who deny life itself. And only he will deny life who has had a painful experience he could not cope with and holds it against the world. Human life is spirit, and in our soul we find ourselves. Once this self-discovery has been achieved, we no longer need to reject any of our experiences; we can find ~~a~~ purpose and meaning in anything happening to us.

Religious communities do have their place and significance in the world of holistic consciousness. They can create places and structures for concentrated reflection of and getting in touch with the spirit. They can cultivate the sensitivity required for nursing and developing the principles of holistic consciousness in any social or cultural sphere. It is their duty to tell the moving tales of their history.

At this stage, however, we can easily do without dogma, without the rigid rules and regulations religious leaders have devised. There will be no stipulated membership; to what or whom we belong is now based on personal relationships rather than institutions. Where people directly experience divinity they need neither institutionalized neither bridges nor official mediators. They will, however, need teachers, role models and inspirators.

Holistic Activity in the Name of Unity

Evolution makes good use of our discontent. Man's discontent is his motivatory factor which allows him to „rest at no place" (Hölderlin) for too long. Of course, we are not just thrown „from rock to rock" passively by the forces of an anonymous development. We can actively take steps, and with each step will we feel more free and confident, if we move in the direction intended by the inner power of evolution. We can trust in the nature of life, which keeps returning to the flow of creative growth as soon as a situation of fear has been mastered. Then the power of evolution may take effect and help consciousness to grow and to flower.

So this is the stage at which we may come to realise what it is that directs and feeds the evolutionary process. It is the same power that directs and feeds *us*. Universalistic consciousness opens the vista of the purpose of social and personal evolution. All that ever came to life and bore fruit at the other stages really sprang from universalistic consciousness.

It is the feeling that we are in the universal flow that at the systemic stage made us happy to serve: serving is simply to contribute to the flow of life and to dedicate one's own contribution to it and to all other living beings.

Earlier stages in the history of evolution are marked by the toils prophesied to man in the book of Genesis. They are stages of fears, but likewise of hopes, which drive us onwards to the next stage. At every new plane of consciousness, we find new treasures, mourning what we have had to leave behind to get to them. On entering a new stage, the mind is expanded. Yet every treasure we find is wound up with a new task, and we will not rest until we have reached the highest plane.

This idea of an ultimate happy ending echoes in all the myths and fairy-tales. It is an idea that originates in the driving power of evolution and leaves our hearts restless (Augustine) until we have found rest in the haven of holistic consciousness.

The religions of previous stages have perpetuated this idea, keeping it alive through the ages. But they also preached that liberation will ensue in the next world or after countless lives that have to be lived for the processing of karma. Materialism bitterly rejected such empty promises and dedicated all its efforts to creating a paradise in this world: the abundance of goods was to ensure happiness in the here and now. By now, of course, this promise of paradise has proven to be no more than a false glint in the eyes of the icons of advertisement. It is now no longer a mystery that in real life happiness does not actually depend on wealth and affluence.

From the materialistic stage we inherit the scepticism that our efforts may never bear fruit, that we will forever be going round in circles or walking along endless straight lines, or that life is just too brief for us ever to find fulfilment. The central theme of the personalistic society is man's coming to terms with the finite nature of his world; it is explored by countless philosophers and artists at this stage. There are, of course, two planes of reality personalistic consciousness cannot quite come to grips with: firstly, the systemic plane, at which all individual endeavours are integrated in a gigantic social web, with unforeseen new possibilities; secondly, the plane of holistic enlightenment, the highest plane, which we all have the basic spiritual potential to climb up to.

Holistic consciousness does not indulge in hypocritical idleness or hermitical retreat. It lives in the midst of the world and pulls up its sleeves. All the suffering in this world must be alleviated.

And for that, holistic consciousness is well equipped. For only if we stay in the present moment and are no longer distracted or inhibited by our fears can we do what is right and expedient. As long as the attention of the agent is wound up exclusively with the past, essential aspects of the present are overlooked. And if our attention is directed solely at the future, we lack the power to recognise what is required of us at the present moment.

One of the paradoxes of holistic consciousness is that by ceasing to attempt to improve the future we may in fact pave the way for a better future. Actions that are in no way influenced by neurotic fears, including those deducted from the uncertainty of the future, are oriented at what the present moment itself has to offer. The ideal strategy for handling a task springs from a communication between the agent and this task that is free from interference.

For holistic action, we rely on the most encompassing view of a situation. As there are no fears that could narrow the field of perception, all that is relevant for assessing the situation is registered by the individual, who acts decisively on the basis of a mature assessment. Thus, reality itself becomes an ally, offering as little resistance as possible to the ongoing activities and providing the energy needed for them.

The more people act in the spirit of holistic awareness, the further will the confidence spread that the consideration of as many interests of other individuals as possible is more worthwhile than the reckless assertion of one's own interests. As human beings, we have a basic, natural interest in the welfare of others. This interest, which is most deeply suppressed at the materialistic stage, takes full effect on the holistic plane. Our trust in unity will flow to places in the soul that were formerly occupied by various fears.

If every moment is appreciated as the most important point in life, whatever is going on in the here and now is no longer essential - drinking a cup of tea is just as valuable as winning the lottery, and washing the dishes is just as important as a ground-breaking invention. If we appreciate each and every activity of ours as valuable, our eyes will be opened to the activities of other people and we will regard them as equals – the road sweeper and the opera diva, the cashier and the bank manager. Thus, we emancipate ourselves from our socially predetermined prejudices, finding it easier to see the inner core of every human being.

This equality should not be confused with indifference or randomness. The problem that systemic consciousness has to battle with is that there can be no absolute point of view from which all developments could be assessed: every assessment is relativised by its own context. We tend to expect other cultures to be quick to take on our own standards of value, and the hypocrisy of this has been unmasked by post-modern relativism. Thus it has become harder to fight human rights violations in other cultures, to decry child labour and the lot of blind infants, who are expelled in Tibetan society. Within the framework of each respective system, what we may classify as a human rights violation is often assessed as a common habit serving the regulation of the social balance.

Holistic consciousness goes one step further. It has in-depth knowledge about every other stage of consciousness. It is capable of identifying the respective historical context of human behaviour while still retaining the overall picture with a view to the highest human potential. This double perspective determines the direction social development will take regarding ethically controversial issues. Regional standards are then examined and improved in exchange with local people.

Holistically motivated action supports this evolutionary perspective, thus weakening circular or reverse processes without having to oppose them violently. It is swept along by the faith that sooner or later the good will win over the bad. This is something worth mobilizing one's energy for.

Overcoming Conflicts of Judgement

Inhibitory factors characteristic for the systemic stage are conflicts of judgement. For the constructivist, it is common practice to take up a contrary position to any given position. The many arguments that are thrown into the ring of systemic intellectual boxing may eventually mar all commitment and lead to an attitude of resignation. The personalistic passion for discussion, for celebrating the great diversity of opinions and viewpoints, which was further encouraged by systemic concepts, is often made into an excuse for idleness or the adoption of cynical attitudes towards life.

For instance, if one person says that eating meat is unhealthy, uneconomical and harmful to the environment, as enormous resources are necessary for the production of animal protein, another will argue that certain indispensable vitamins, mineral salts and trace elements can only be provided via the consumption of meat. Human intelligence itself, he will say, may be attributed to the carnivoracious aspect of our ancestors' diet. Also, we ought to bear in mind the situation of livestock breeders. What to do, then? The superabundance of information we have access to in the age of systemic consciousness paralyses our executive faculties.

At the stage of holistic consciousness, we no longer try to understand or take into consideration every opinion and every piece of information we come across. We realise that the human *mind* – though infinitely capable of learning – is limited in its structure. The human *soul*, on the other hand, being capable of connecting with everything in existence, is limitless by nature.

The mind, which since the materialistic stage has dominated the scene (Descartes: *cogito, ergo sum*), is now assigned the humble place of the advisor of a vast consciousness, asked to consider relevant information and make comments whenever necessary. Even though the decisions resulting from this are often rationally comprehensible, they are always grounded in the secret of oneness. The motives for our actions are not derived from the databases of the mind but from the abundance of the soul. They are not determined by egocentric attitudes or unconscious fears but feed on the inexhaustible wisdom of this abundance.

Therefore, one who is steeped in holistic consciousness does not think in terms of "wrong" or "right". Every action leads to its consequence, and this consequence is consistent. Every action springs from an unconditional acceptance of what is.

The essential things in life reveal themselves by themselves, as we have given them enough room; we do not need to make a great effort to discover them.

If we fully trust holistic oneness, no monitoring will be required. Of course, at the holistic stage the authorities of control, which have been incorporated into organisations since the stage of hierarchical consciousness, will continue to exist so as to safeguard against regression into pre-holistic circumstances. However, they will be activated only if such a regression is actually taking place. Their own conduct is determined by holistic principles; they perform their duties with an attitude of good will and integrity and not out of power-political motives.

On the basis of this, the problem of evil solves itself. In the state of holistic awareness, it does not seem to make a lot of sense to lament about suffering. We have different experiences, pleasant or unpleasant. There is nothing good or evil about this. In all areas of nature some processes are successful and others fail (one seed drops to fertile ground and grows, another shrinks up and dies). Man, too, either fulfils his destiny or fails to do so, and either (and everything in between) is accepted impartially for what it is. There are no more absolute contrasts, only transitions from one empirical reality to the next, displaced by nuances and shades, not separated from each other by categories.

Evil now appears as a problem of the human mind, which extends its database of evaluation to all known phenomena. For anything that happens, or rather for anything we experience, it may put a mark on the scale between good and evil. This causes additional suffering: the unpleasant experiences life will confront us with are supplied with debasement, so that we are not only disturbed by our experience but burden ourselves with negative judgement.

Wherever suffering has ceased to exist because there is no judgementalism, evil loses its power as well. If a wise woman is done wrong – if she is, say, cheated –, she does not suffer but treats the incident simply as another experience and carries on with an attitude of equanimity. (Just as a less wise person may years later look back on such an experience without experiencing pain, anger, or desire for vengeance.) The wise woman will feel compassion for the wrongdoer, whose hopelessness it was that led to the harmful and loveless deed. She, however, also expects of him to bear the consequences of his action.

If the wise woman turns ill and has to endure physical pain, she does not suffer emotionally because she accepts even the unpleasant and unbearable aspects of the experience and is therefore able to be in inner harmony with herself and with life.

At a social level, what people do to other people is dealt with by the authorities responsible. The more people attain a state of holistic wisdom, the further evil will retreat. Only one who is driven by fear will do his fellow human beings wrong. The essential chore is then to contribute to the elimination of fear. This also entails commitment to the cause of reforming unjust, exploitative structures causing fear.

One who is in the state of holistic consciousness is, then, free from the drive of wishing or doing other people wrong. She is capable of disregarding personal advantages and of focussing on viewing the whole picture rather than only aspects. She is free to look at issues from different angles. She assesses her own actions at reality and her experiences. She examines her own judgements and biases and may easily let go of them. She is not susceptible to material temptations and does not strive for power. She nurses a deep longing for universal happiness. This is someone we may refer to as a person of integrity. She is in tune with herself and free from conditionings and images, so that she is not determined in her actions by ingrained emotions but makes the best of every situation.

It takes such people to provide holistic consciousness with a strong foundation. They serve as role models, helping us to orient ourselves in this post-modern age of relativity and randomness. Whoever trusts the power of systemic consciousness will also confide in these people; and thus, quite magically, the most suitable people move to the positions where decisions are made.

People of integrity also serve as teachers for those caught up in their fears, showing them ways of conquering them and of establishing their own integrity. They take care that organisations maintain their integrity and that the structures are kept free from patterns causing fear. They are mediators of social development; they register and pinpoint the weak points and indurations of public discourse.

If the bad disappears at the holistic stage, does that mean that everything will hover in a non-judgemental space, where not even the good can be perceived? According to the logic of nature, which has provided organisms with a growth state for normal situations and a protective state for situations of emergency, we see that the good is only possible if the bad makes room for it. Just as the temptation for theft grows weaker with the spreading of prosperity, the inclination for evil will or deed fades where inner peace and harmony prevail. This holds true both for groups and for cultures.

The further we evolve towards holistic consciousness, the more good things will happen in this world, whether in smaller contexts or in larger ones. One day there will be no more people who would willingly choose evil instead of good. It will not be a world in which everything is perfect and all the people live together in constant harmony. But it will be a world in which human cruelty is reduced so far as to ensure that such imperfections be processed and dissolved timely and without their causing lasting damage.

Just as we have learnt to quickly repair a damage we encounter in our material environment (fixing, for instance, a hole in the roof for the rain not to get in), we will learn to quickly and effectively redress the damage we have caused on a communicative or ethical level, so that the evil, wherever it occurs, may be stemmed and disempowered by an atmosphere of respect and love.

The Simplitude of Truth

As yet, we may not register a great many cases of fully realised holistic consciousness. The fundamental statements of the holistic stage as such, however, are convincing to a great number of people, as they refer to a plausible interpretation of reality. Who would reject a statement like, "Love thy neighbour as thyself"? Who would not feel relieved on hearing, "It is best to accept everything the way it is"?

The only problem is that this simplicity is difficult to apply to our everyday life and bring in tune with its ever greater complexities. "How can I practise loving my neighbour when the streets are full of beggars?" "How can I accept everything the way it is when others have hurt me in this way or that?"

Up to now, all we can refer to is practice fields for this stage of consciousness in certain segments of the developing societies. There are communities living by the principles of truthfulness and honesty; there are circles in which unconditional respect for others is fostered; meetings where in an atmosphere of freedom all animosity and fault-finding must wait outside the door. These practice fields show the participants how deeply liberating and nourishing such experiences are and let them experience the contrast to aspects of reality still dominated by other levels of consciousness.

Every stage begins with little steps and is at first sneered at or threatened by predominant consciousness. It is quite understandable that, within the context of a predominant paradigm, one might not see clearly what it is that can cure present ills. Fears that ensure the inner connectedness of a certain level of consciousness are projected onto anything that promises solution.

It is, then, hardly possible to say what will be the central ideas and strategies of a society that has broken free from the compelling basic fears of earlier stages of consciousness and has developed a deeper understanding of the connectedness of all creation. The fears characteristic for the respective stages serve as putty for them, and the members of these communities are impregnated with these fears, so that already in their mother's womb they built up tensions that will seem as natural to them as breathing. As soon as they are born they start contributing to the mutual increase and confirmation of fearful expectations. Wherever we manage to break these cycles, new windows towards holistic consciousness open up and forces we have hitherto been ignorant of are employed to create something new.

Systemic consciousness knows of the infinite complexity not only of the world but of its meaning. In holistic consciousness, this recognition becomes the treasure of man, who has learnt to bear the tension between complexity and simplicity and to handle it playfully.

While systemic consciousness, with its enormous desire for knowledge, used to urge from one level of complexity to the next, holistic consciousness rediscovers simplicity in the richness of the present moment. It is a world where people may study in depth any form of complexity, knowing that it is all down to games they can but do not have to play and may stop playing anytime – that is, if for want of enjoyment or benefit they cease to be pleasurable or if they promise no further benefit. Complexity in its manifold forms in science, arts, philosophy, technology and social manners serves as a playing field for the mind with the purpose of enriching human life.

Referring to the centre, that which all human endeavour is ultimately bent on, one is all too easily misunderstood. The formulations one might fall back on have been used so many times before to describe and propagate the relative centres of previous stages. Every tradition has attributed these formulations to other contexts so that a contradictory texture of theories ensnares an undefinable centre.

If, for instance, the centre is referred to as "God" and someone claims that there is only one God who cannot be depicted, another person will dispute this saying that God is really three persons, one of whom brought the message to the world. A third individual will insist that the saviour has not come yet, because salvation has never happened.

Thus, positions will contrast, every one of them being presented with commitment and credibility. No one is wrong, no one alone is right.

The fights and contradictions all belong to the forecourt of the sanctuary. Within the sanctuary itself there is silence and immersedness. And those who wish to enter the sanctuary must leave behind the trouble and strife and be prepared to embrace every other position. Otherwise, they will not be able to experience the tranquillity in which the sacred is revealed.

Ken Wilber rightly states that every stage of consciousness develops its own views of the absolute and that misunderstandings and fights largely result from the fact that the conflicting parties do not reveal from which level of consciousness they speak and argue. He also showed that it is best to accompany a statement with the specification how one got to it. The idea of the absolute, then, is pure - that is, free from culture-specific bias – only if it is formulated from a position that has experienced all the stages of the evolution of consciousness, having reached, in our terminology, the seventh stage of evolution.

The sober language employed by systemic consciousness has the purpose of making acceptable systemic ideas and the results of systemic thinking to the possible circle of recipients. Systemic consciousness is indebted to the paradigm of modern science, which requires the universal communicability of the scientific texts on the basis of scientific rationality.

Holistic consciousness may respect all scientifically backed results. However, its duty is not to engage in scientific or ideological quarrels to defend its positions, as will some representatives of religious communities (concerning, for instance, Darwin's evolutionary theory) or proponents of esoteric views (generalising certain findings in quantum physics in support of their own views). While respecting the sciences, holistic consciousness is not stuck with its ways of gaining insights. Also, the strict empirical and mathematical criteria of science cannot be applied to holistic thought and experience. Holistic experiences per se cannot be generalised. Also, they are not comprehensive to anybody at any given time. On the contrary, the experiences that open the door to holistic consciousness are unique and cannot be reproduced in a scientific sense.

Therefore, the language of this stage is colourful, poetic and free, paradoxical and imminently convincing. Talk is of unconditional love, infinite happiness, and all-encompassing unity.

The Experience of Time

The history of evolution is characterised by an enormous acceleration of time. In the beginnings of the evolution of life it took millions of years for a new evolutionary level – for instance, that of bilaterally symmetric living beings) – to be reached. For millions of years, people lived in tribal communities, and for thousands they were steeped in the ancient civilisations. The industrial age lasted for hundreds of years, and the age of highly advanced technology so far has been going on for just a few decades. Social forms like the extended family, which for thousands of years had been the centre of people's lives, disappear within a relatively short space of time, and new social forms of organisation such as bachelor pads and patchwork families spread just as quickly.

Our concept of time has changed accordingly. Imagine what the sense of time of the early life forms might have been like, when mankind had millions of years to practise a new way of being. Today fashions, forms of communication, lifestyles, and cultural contexts change over years or even months. More and more people feel that time is finite and short. In addition, the ideology of shortage of materialism has impregnated this acceleration with fear. Time is running out, is the motto of that epoch. Time is measured as precisely as ever before, so that we may register every detail in the process of its disappearance, without being able to do anything about it.

Personalistic thinking has opposed the fury of the industrial age with the reflection on the finite nature of life. This, however, would merely point out absolute limits for the unbridled acceleration, only heightening the pressure in this life of completing tasks within ever shorter time periods. Given that my life is restricted to an uncertain count of years, I must strive to fill that time with as many meaningful activities as possible. The fear of death, which intrudes on personalistic man, is the gear for his race against time.

This acceleration cannot be stopped by the means of systemic consciousness. It may be possible to introduce systems in a decelerated manner or to include braking mechanisms, but those are only marginal compared to the insight into the limitedness of life on this planet, which encourage an even greater exploitation of ever fewer temporal resources.

It is only in the light of holistic consciousness that the permeation of time with the stage-specific fears becomes transparent and can ultimately be overcome. When there is no more fear, time, too, ceases to exist. All that matters is the present moment. If change is experienced as a continuous flow of different present moments, we no longer need to think of categories like future and past. Time will then stand still in the present moment.

The mind cannot remain permanently in a state of holistic consciousness. The requirements of practical life demand us to return to a linear concept of time. Planning and communicative coordination with other people, supply activities and breadwinning all take place within a traditional time structure. But this time structure is recognised as a temporary, not as an all-dominating reality and is used only to organise life on a practical level.

We can only speculate as to what will happen to a society where holistic consciousness had reached a critical mass. Time as a concept would certainly become less relevant and would have to forego the dictatorial role we frequently grant it. "Have you got some time?" "Well, I've got the present moment, it is my very own..."

Systems have an inert tendency towards optimisation. Internal processes adjust themselves to one another until a balance is created that may become obsolete the very next moment. This orientation at a solution sticks to the idea of a time line, along which experiences of the past can be made useful for working towards a future goal. Whenever time is imagined as a line, fear is involved: I will think of something that happened in the past because I do not want to make the same mistake again; I will plan for the future to prevent something from happening to me that I have suffered before. Our striving for a solution, for which we make efforts within our system, is motivated by our desire to soothe our fears.

In holistic consciousness the time line collapses, as there are no more old fears. There are no more problems to solve: instead, perfection is appreciated in the present moment. The beauty of the present appears as the heart of reality once the fears that shrouded it have fallen away.

Integrating Earlier Stages of Consciousness

Evolution has not gone through six stages to leave them behind and forget them. From the point of view of the seventh stage, as we have mentioned, every earlier plane retains its own dignity and its own value. As becomes apparent in holistic consciousness, it is of great importance for universal coherence that all areas of human life be managed by the means of the stage of consciousness most suitable for it.

The tribal plane is best when it comes to ritual and shamanistic healing. This is also what it contributes to the world's spiritual development. The emancipatory plane retains the spirit of initiative and departure. The hierarchical stage has had the most detailed experiences regarding social rules and regulations, authority, and the administration of power. The materialistic stage has acquired the greatest skills regarding the handling of money, business, production, and resources. The personalistic stage is responsible for handling the problems and entanglements of the individual soul. Systemic consciousness regulates complex processes in all other systems and makes sure that ethical standards are respected.

It makes no sense, therefore, to contaminate the holistic sphere with the values and processes of monetary economics. It must remain independent of them. Spiritual teachers may fail in drawing lines between the holistic and the materialistic sphere, whether it is by making a fortune by their teachings or by in no way taking care of that sphere and expecting to be supported by "existence".

"Render unto Caesar that which is Caesar's and unto God that which is God's", so it is said in the Bible. Financial matters are financial matters, and spiritual matters are spiritual matters. Financial matters are dealt with on the materialistic plane, spiritual ones on the holistic plane. Questions of power or ethical matters are analogous cases.

Indeed, if conflicts or problems of clarity cannot be solved by the means of a certain current stage, it may become necessary to fall back on the knowledge and the insights of other stages. Superordinate systems have evolved because the pressing questions of a stage could not be solved by the means of that same stage. But whatever can be solved at a subordinate plane, should be solved there. A great deal of confusion will arise if the superiority of a certain stage is projected back onto the duties and the problems of earlier stages, as if it could there change anything that seems unpleasant or inappropriate. So it was, for instance, with the European conquerors overseas, who thought they had to do everything in their power to help the natives, who had lived together in relative harmony for hundreds of years, to the benefits of Christianity and occidental civilisation.

Every stage of consciousness involves a tendency towards the universal, which is expressed in different forms of transcendence and spirituality. At any time, single individuals may have holistic experiences. They are shamans or wizards in tribal cultures, founders of religions at the emancipatory stage, saints and prophets in the structures of hierarchical consciousness, hermits at the materialistic and wisdom teachers at the personalistic stage.

At every stage, however, there is likewise the temptation to abuse holistic insights for the selfish ends of the powerful. There are false prophets and war-hungry priests, gods or demi-gods on thrones, and manipulators "dis-guised as heaven" at every level of society.

Stage seven of the evolution of consciousness does not contribute new technologies, methods, structures, or organisations. It is not based on clever inventions and refined processes, and does not triumph with artistic innovations and brilliant ideas. Instead, it guarantees universal integrity and harmony. Our journey through the stages of evolution has shown that at every stage solutions are found that create new problems. Through holistic consciousness it becomes clear that overlooking or forgetting the universal dimension will cause separation, individualisation, and isolation. The cause of human suffering is the dissociation from universal unity, which develops fully at the holistic stage.

If society is ready to move towards the holistic stage with greater momentum, then the necessaries for ensuring survival and social balance have already been fulfilled by what mankind achieved at the earlier stages. Not before the universal point of view is taken can they be filled with meaning. Otherwise, every technology, every method, every breakthrough will remain an isolated piece and could be the cause of confusion and destruction. As a yardstick, the holistic point of view is indispensable, if of all the creative power that the human race has displayed since its beginnings, the best for all living things is to come.

Striving for Holistic Consciousness

Many people have had holistic experiences. Most of the time, they are accompanied with feelings of happiness and inner peace. They may manifest themselves when we are close to nature or are enjoying art, when we feel in tune with other human beings or are delving deep into the heart. We may assume that such experiences are transient and require unusual circumstances to occur. In fact, they point to the tremendous potential that is hidden inside us, waiting to be revealed and fully realised.

What can we do to strengthen and heighten the power of holistic consciousness in our hearts? How can we find the inner peace we long for? How can we give the world our best? Here are a couple of simple suggestions, whose regular following may serve this purpose.

Exercises

Being in the Present Moment

Instructions: If you watch your breath, you will always be in the present moment. Your breath is the clearest bodily function that can always be observed. It shows you how you feel at a certain moment. Watch your breath as it flows in and out. This is how you live right now, at this moment, flowing freely or in a manner of restrictedness, big or small, open or retreated. Accept the way you are and feel at this moment; it is all right. It will change soon, and that, too, is all right. The inbreath teaches you that this moment holds a wealth of power for you to draw on; the outbreath teaches you that you can let go of and give away all you no longer need.

If you feel tense and out of balance in everyday life, then this is a good opportunity to watch your breath and to relax as you are breathing out. This is how you may easily find yourself, letting go of the worries and burdens that are troubling you at the moment. You will recognise that every moment has a special gift to offer, which you can cherish.

Peak Experiences

Instructions: Can you recall ever to have had the heavenly feeling that within you and without you everything is in tune? This experience frequently occurs when we are close to nature. You may have it when after a long hike you reach a peak (hence the term peak experience), or if you are sitting in a beautiful place, thinking of nothing but the awesome view exposed to you – a moment you wish would not pass.

As you try to recall such an experience, can you also remember the feeling you had at that moment? You may think that this feeling was due to external circumstances – the landscape around you, the activity you engaged in at the time, etc. – and that you will therefore never relive that experience. How about this: at that moment you discovered something that has always been there and that is just waiting for you to let it happen again!

What if this is true? Would it motivate you to look for ways to make peak experiences part of your everyday emotional routine? Would you then wish that more people partook in such experiences? And would you ask yourself how you could help them in this matter?

The Compassion Exercise

Instructions: Sit in a relaxed manner while still trying to keep your back straight. Now close your eyes. Let your breath flow easily. Focus on the gentle motion of your breath – as it flows in ... and as it flows out.

Now think of the suffering in your environment, and imagine that you imbibe this suffering with your inbreath, allowing it to flow into your heart. From there, breathe out and send love and light to those who are suffering. Do this practice for a few minutes, until you feel that love and light alone are flowing from your heart.

Then widen the circle to your country, then to the entire earth, then to the entire cosmos.

* * *

The practices of holistic consciousness are the gifts from the path of meditation. This path may lead to tranquillity, relaxation, and profound insights. You will feel that there is a path to liberation and may look for appropriate support along this path or feel gratitude for the help you have so far been given.

The Vista of a Global Community

„You may say that I'm a dreamer, but I'm not the only one."
(John Lennon)

If we consider the current state of affairs around the world in combination with the model of the evolution of consciousness, some conclusions seem to beg themselves. They are not of the order of prophecies but derive from the tendencies humankind has displayed over the thousands of years of its existence. Despite many examples of evil twists and relapses, there has been a slow qualitative development to the positive. In the light of this, it does not seem altogether presumptuous to contemplate bold, but equally realistic, dreams about the future.

It is evident that many of the developments of our day will cause damage either in the short or in the long run, aggravating old problems and creating new ones. If we take a closer look at these tendencies, it will become clear that they result from deeply engrained modes of thinking determined by largely subconscious fears. The many structural constraints the global community feels imprisoned in are like generalised neurotic conflicts indicating that the evolution of consciousness stagnated in places, causing internal and external perception to differ substantially. The resulting feelings of tension are acted out collectively, thus causing the evils that hurt the global community. In many places, attachment to selfish interests dictates the course society takes. A people will vote for or tolerate an administration that works in opposition to its needs and its hopes for the future. Systems of power cannot be overcome by means of power; stubbornness does not defeat stubbornness. Therefore, it is a further development of consciousness that is needed to transform dead ends into gateways to the liberation of man from unnecessary ills. We cannot derive from our model how long it will take for each step to be completed. The figures we might give would be a matter of mere speculation. What we may, however, deduct is that sooner or later these changes will actually occur; the earlier, the better for our world.

Conclusion One: A Global Government

The problems of our world can be solved only if we introduce a global government with the power and competences it needs to assert itself. The monopoly on force, then, must pass to this global government. Nation states will lose their sovereignty and surrender much of their power. Essentially, this is only the continuation on a larger scale of a process that began during the transition period between stage 3 and stage 4 hundreds of years ago. Nowadays, luckily, it is perfectly common in many parts of the world that a quarrel between neighbours be settled by a judge or a mediator rather than decided by armed force. Analogously, future generations will know of war only what their elders tell them about it, being glad that this is so.

Nation states will renounciate their right to absolute rulership only if this is to their own advantage. International communities such as the European Union have demonstrated that such a renunciation can be advantageous on many levels. Renunciation, however, is possible only if the new superordinate structure is bound to a superordinate wisdom and its representatives command unquestionable integrity. Members of a global government should then have cultivated this quality. They should be of a systemic mind and steeped in holistic consciousness, having internalised an attitude of devotion and servitude (which, in the end, benefits them as well). They should command the wisdom and intelligence it takes to carefully balance conflicts of interest; and they should be capable of asserting themselves to keep personal interests within bounds.

There is an example that may illustrate the workings of such a government. Let us imagine a future where there is only one government, one parliament, one Supreme Court in the world. Backed by the parliament, the government sets itself the task of resolving the conflict in the Near East. It is of the opinion that over the decades this conflict has caused a great deal of misery, suffering and distress, and that nothing should be left untried to reach a resolution. Also, it recognises that local politicians and rulers are unable to make peace voluntarily. Finally, it is convinced that conflicts will consume great amounts of resources, which by far exceed the costs of solid peace regulations.

First, all armed groups and local armies involved are demanded to hand over their weapons to the global executive body. If the warring factions will not commit themselves voluntarily to the peace process, they are invited to a conference, which will be held until they come to an agreement. All local non-governmental organisations committed to the cause of peace participate in this conference. There are prominent participants and representatives „of the people". There are mixed groups, with hosts making sure that a process of communication happens between the parties. In these groups, people relate their experiences, what they have suffered and feared; and the hosts make sure that people listen and that accusations are avoided. In this way, systemic and holistic consciousness are practised.

If during the conference there has been a shift in people's opinions and if this changed perspective has been fairly established in them, then the time will come when the major representatives of the warring factions are ready to relinquish power and end the violence. Then the global government will take control of the military of the region concerned, in continuous correspondence with the local authorities, so that this rule may be just. With the local groups being no longer permitted to revert to violent means, fear declines within the community. Perpetrators against this prohibition are punished no matter which side they are on.

In another step, the material living conditions must be levelled to such an extent as to ensure that all social groups have enough resources so as not to have an objective cause to fear for their own survival. The infrastructure is improved accordingly. As it is a project of the global government, there are enough financial resources available to make this possible.

Once people's living conditions in the crisis zone have been established at a reasonable level, a great number of local conferences are held, for which people from opposing groups come together to talk. As with the above-mentioned disarming conference, the dialogue is conducted by international hosts. Those who are prepared to contribute to the peace process are compensated by the global government for investing their time, so that everyone may have the chance to participate. The people involved will talk about the things important to them, about their families, their history, their values and their religion. They will hear what other people have experienced and how they have suffered. In an atmosphere of fearlessness, they will learn to understand the people on the other side.

The hope is that as many people as possible will join the conference, yet participation is basically voluntary. The more people taste of systemic and holistic consciousness, the further the peaceable atmosphere will spread among the peoples concerned. In the course of the process of dialogue, the settling of legal matters, such as the question of land ownership, of dispossessions, etc., is prepared. There will be common courts, in which the local judges of both sides administer justice – if necessary, with international support.

Throughout this process, all stages of consciousness are respected. The needs from the various planes of consciousness are understood on both sides; they are mutually respected and appreciated.

This process is continued until the global government is convinced that the foundations have been laid out for a peace lasting for years or decades.

This is how a global community of the future may go about resolving the tenacious socio-political conflicts of the world: or it may implement even better plans to tackle them. Is that mere fantasy, folly, or fanciful idealism?

People who have always been living in warlike, violent climates cannot easily switch to attitudes necessary for the peace process. In order to acquire them they must abandon the violent contexts and accept the advice of people who are themselves not involved in the conflicts. Otherwise, it is hardly conceivable for the hatred to retreat from people's hearts and minds. And it is hatred that eats up the soul. The deepest longing we carry within our hearts is for liberation from hatred, fear and suffering. And it is to this end that we should devote our efforts as a species. As far as I am concerned, this insight is more real than any of the arguments that might be put against the ideas formulated above.

Conclusion Two: Equal Opportunities

Differences regarding opportunities must be levelled. All the people that, given their social and economic circumstances, still linger at earlier stages of consciousness push for a broader spectrum of possibilities. Everyone should be able to enjoy the positive achievements of bureaucracy (social security), materialism (affluence) and personality (freedom).

In the context of different stages of consciousness, there will be ratchet effects, which result in the fact that no one will voluntarily surrender the achievements of historical development she is enjoying but wants more of them. This effect is most evident at the plane of materialism with regard to the numerical principle. The ascending numerical sequence being limitless, there can be no "enough". One can have enough to eat, there is a limit beyond which the body will eject what it is given. There is, however, no point where one has enough money or goods. Why shouldn't someone who has ten million want to make it twelve million, and once he has got them, even more? Why shouldn't someone who has two cars want to possess a third one, and, once he has got it, to own yet another? This spiral of greed can be broken only on the inside. Every limitation from the outside is aimed at breaking the inside, which defends itself at every cost.

The necessary self-restriction is the result of a change of consciousness. When a new plane of inner organisation is reached, what seemed important before is re-interpreted and loses some of its appeal. The fears that hitherto caused us to be greedy are then no longer relevant, and suddenly the object of our burning desire loses its attraction to us. Just like an addict who has come to understand and broken the mechanisms of self-injury can turn to better ways of living, so will the members of affluent societies be able to bridle their excessive consumption habits if they comprehend and overcome the perpetual mechanisms of consumptive behaviour. If the affluent societies realise that on the road to liberation via personal growth, systemic virtue and holistic experience they will much more substantially acquire health and joie de vivre than by buying and destroying goods, they will voluntarily reduce their demands and thus their over proportional part in global consumption.

This self-restriction in the rich creates new opportunities for the poor for nourishment and cure of ailments. If this transition is to be successful to such an extent as to ensure the equal distribution of wealth over the world population, a great measure of systemic wisdom is required in the places of decision-making. New modes of logistic planning will have to be developed to achieve this end of universal interest.

Compulsory measures can at best play a subjugated role here. Therefore, these changes cannot manifest before an inner transformation has happened and the processes of change are supported by the people.

Everyone will benefit: the rich because they are able to let go of their fear and leave behind their woes in the clockworks of consumerism, and the poor because they are enabled to enjoy elementary security and the satisfaction of their needs. They can then more quickly pass through the stages of evolution, not having to suffer unnecessarily in the pitfalls of growth, contemplating the mistakes of their predecessors. It is to be hoped that the poor societies of today will pass the materialistic stage at a pace that the eco-system will still be able to handle. Many societies of the third and fourth worlds have not lost their connection to tribal and hierarchical forms of spirituality to such a great extent as the West has done. It may therefore prove easier for them to see through and move beyond the limits of wealth and affluence.

Conclusion Three: Nature and Creativity

The relationship between man and nature will become a harmonious one. Improving their attitude towards their own body, they lay out an inner foundation for respect of nature. The materialistic trap of self-exploitation, which in spite of its changed form can still be seen at the personalistic stage, blocks the experience that the human race is inevitably connected with nature. When we turn ill and weak, the glow of wealth will melt like snow in the sun. And physical damage, damage done to nature of our own, is inevitable if we expose ourselves to more stress than we can handle.

The way out of the trap of self-exploitation is in resolving the fears that drive us to burdening ourselves with stress, thus causing a downward spiral of fear. The fear buried inside us weakens our vital energy and wears out our most precious vital powers. It is therefore of great importance that we re-establish our close relationship with nature, through conscious breathing and other strategies for relieving stress that human creativity has devised. Respecting the wisdom of the body instead of exploiting our physical resources will make us rich and creative, strong and free.

If we were to apply this idea on a global level, it would mean that, following the resolution of certain collective fears weakening the connection, the human race will establish a deeper and more cooperative relationship with nature. The collective stress of the global community and the accelerating processes of mechanisation must be reduced so man will not end up as a victim of himself. Nature follows analogous rhythms, which are neither perfectly constant nor perfectly exact but which neatly adapt to the course of events. Nature, thus, understands time as something in a flow. Our body, being of the same disposition, will suffer if it is subjected to an alien digital time structure. Stress is created where something is supposed to happen at a very particular point in time and if this in no way corresponds to the inner rhythm of the organism.

Moreover, digital time structures can easily be accelerated. A piece of music that has been recorded digitally can, without the change of another parameter, be played in double speed (how about a one-minute's waltz in 30 seconds?). Analogous organic procedures can be accelerated only for a limited duration and then require a phase of regeneration.

It seems that the mechanisation and capitalisation of the world, i.e. the mechanical world view, involves a dynamic of acceleration. This dynamic is very subtle, taking place below the stimulus threshold, in fact, so that under normal circumstances we are not aware of it. If we receive a delivery just at the time we were reckoning with, we are content, otherwise we will quickly become angry. Greater precision requires yet greater precision; so that timekeeping will become ever so exact, from telling times of the day such as morning, noon and evening to hours, minutes, and seconds.

This is just one example of how we can learn from nature to find ourselves again. We must find ways of restricting the processes based on acceleration, so that our organisms will be exposed to them only for a limited duration every time and we may more often follow analogous time structures, which allow for relaxation.

Regaining awareness of these mechanisms of regulation is building a new foundation for our relationship with nature and thus taking a first step in opposition to the destruction of life on this planet. An inwardly balanced body is in tune with nature, deepening its awareness of it. When this tremendous power, this dazzling diversity and beauty of nature becomes an integral part of our inner experience again, this will motivate us to act in accordance with nature and its processes. If we commit ourselves to systemic consciousness, this form of integral unity with a more encompassing reality will become accessible to us.

At the collective plane, this leap forward in development is prepared for in two ways. The inner dynamic of industrial society and its forms of organisation requires systemic thinking at all levels. Capitalism can only survive if it is converted to systemic ideals. Systemic consciousness, however, has a dynamic of relentless expansion and will therefore sooner or later come to encompass the systems of nature. Already there are first signs to this effect: some companies creating their products in the classical fields of industry will devote part of their capacities to nature-related projects.

The other form of preparation is revealed in the passing of consciousness from materialism over personalism to the systemic stage. The respect for the individual in the explicit formulation of human rights is extended to respect for nature, whose own rights are more and more often claimed. The more we learn about ourselves, the more profound will be our experience that everything that happens within or without is controlled by an all-encompassing and all-affecting intelligence. We will experience that it is enough to entrust oneself to this ever-benevolent intelligence, which leads nature and man to the best of the whole.

Conclusion Four: Diversity

The world of the future will be yet more colourful and diverse than our day. The webs of communication will be spun even more densely and more variedly all around the globe. The binding power of tribal roots will thus be loosened up even further, and national identifications will become more and more brittle. People will meet people in real and virtual forums, with national identities playing very little or no role.

All cultural traditions will be treated with equal respect and attention, incorporated in a common fund and accepted wholeheartedly. At all levels of artistic and media production, the creative ideas will be drawn from the plentiful sources of the diverse cultures of the world, giving rise to many delightful innovations.

This is how people may put in their hearts appreciation of and joy about otherness and keep it safely enshrined there. Otherness is no longer interpreted as dangerous, becoming instead the object of wonder and learning. Just as more and more people become globetrotters, who, starting in a certain culture, move on and on, so do cultural goods travel around the world, becoming richer with every new station. This world of creative flow needs neither violence nor hatred to produce excitement but enjoys the variedness of human creative power and the traditions it brings forth. Thus, this world is connected through a highly active network of multilingual narratives, which, according to individual taste or interest, may be entered by anyone from any point, to receive or create. This is the genesis of the cultural citizens of the world of the future, for whom national or racial prejudices are merely relicts of the past.

The quality of playfulness is given independent justifiability to the extent at which the dominance of the concept of performance is curtailed. Status and prestige are no longer determined by economic success alone. The "width" of a person – that is, the extent to which one is able to unfold personal inner capacities – will be increasingly at the heart of character assessment. One aspect of personal width is a creative relationship towards purpose-free spheres. A game with its diverse options serves not only as a means of relaxation or communication but as revival of one's inner freedom and revaluation of one's childlike aspects. Even institutions and organisations will recognise that innovation, productivity and contentment may increase if we cultivate purpose-free spheres.

The dominance of single information centres will pass for the sake of greater diversity. As the technologies of the future are increasingly adaptable and more and more easy to handle, they will be usable and available throughout the world, and everywhere to the same extent. The level of education will rise so high that such technologies can be created and improved anywhere in the world. Creative products from all over the world could then be made use of and enjoyed. The entertainment industry will go universalistic. Every place on Earth will make its contribution to world culture, which will resemble a giant, ever-changing carpet containing all colours and shades. Every detail will be the source of surprise and wonder.

Appendix

Other Models of Evolution

On the Concept by Ken Wilber

Ken Wilbers comprehensive representation of the phenomena of human consciousness serves as a good framework for these considerations. In my opinion, the ideas introduced here are compatible with it. As model of stages of consciousness, they fit in the theoretical framework. For reasons of simplicity, we have subsumed the final (most highly developed) stages of Wilber's model of the evolution of consciousness (turquois to violet) under one (stage 7).

Insofar as Ken Wilber by and large remains faithful to the model of spiral dynamics by Clare Graves and his disciples Don Beck and Chris Cowan, the deviations I will be elaborating on are also valid in comparison with Wilber's meta-model.

Differences to the Model of Spiral Dynamics (Graves, Beck and Cowan)

In all thankful appreciation for everything that I owe to the model of my intellectual forerunners, my study of the subject has lead me to deviating insights, which are as follows.

Difference 1: Stage 1 Is Omitted.

Graves begins with a stage of individual struggle for survival. It seems unrealistic to me that the beginning of human evolution should be single individuals striving to ensure their own survival. Men have always lived in groups, just like their closest relatives, the primates. It is absolutely characteristic of the early human beings with their lack of instinct that they could ensure survival only while remaining within groups. Therefore, individual survival should always be seen as parallel to group survival.

It is now known that man has no isolated drive for survival which comes first before social needs, although other theories of evolution, such as Maslow's "hierarchy of needs" or Loevinger's theory of personality, reason from the presumption of primary individual survival. One the contrary, the results of studies on new-born babies done over the last 20 years, which have identified the new-born child as an actively communicating being, are a point against the idea of an overruling individual drive for survival. In addition, study on mirror neurons has revealed that man possesses cerebral structures that constantly establish and stabilise connections with other human beings.

Thus, humans have been communicators from their beginnings (whether from new-born babies or from hominids) and as such are in constant exchange with their environment, seeking contact and communication. It is only in extreme situations that our survival mechanism, as mobilised by fear, will predominate and isolate us. In our "normal state", which alone ensures survival in the long run, we will function and grow in a communicative field that connects us with our environment.

Therefore, it should seem awkward to put at the very beginning of human existence a state of individual survival, as if man were a single being that out of mere necessity will turn into a social creature and may at any time return to the original status of lone wolf existence. This view is the basis of many unfortunate ideologies and is not in line with the scientific findings of recent years. The reason why this view of man as basically "going it alone" has remained so prevalent is due to the predominance of materialistic and personalistic consciousness in our day. If we can avoid viewing cultural evolution through those lenses, we will find that "the solitary" is an abstraction, not a fundamental reality or the basis of evolution. Much rather can we identify the plane of consciousness with its specific requirements that brings forth such a view. Following the narrow pass this idea of man led to, consciousness climbs to the next stage.

In this representation, organic consciousness is also referred to in the beginning. It is not called the initial stage of cultural evolution, but certain determinants that are encoded in the basic processes of life seemed essential to the understanding of cultural evolution, so I chose to mention them. How people "function", then, is partly due to the basic patterns of life *per se*. These are discussed briefly but in such a way that the average person may understand.

Difference 2: Foregoing Colour Assignments

Graves and his disciples use colour to mark the individual stages. This was done to prevent the hierarchical evaluation that would have occurred if the stages had been assigned numbers, as many people would have thought that a stage was the better the higher its number was. They believed that as far as the further development from one stage to another is concerned we cannot speak of improvements, only of new adaptations to new problems.

In the evolution of stages, I do not see a fundamentally infinite sequence of cognitive principles of organisation and value structures (^{V}MEME in Spiral Dynamics, V standing for value) but a consistent upward development with an inner logic, comparable to the stages if moral development by Lawrence Kohlberg, where one stage is the prerequisite for another. A later stage is "higher" than an earlier stage insofar as it has integrated and can apply certain learning experiences.

I wish to expose the logical consistency inherent in evolution so that the coincidentialities may be revealed as an aspect of limited viewpoints evoked by the limitations of individual stages of consciousness. New perspectives of orientation and patterns of behaviour are improvements insofar as they rework and reframe the insufficient aspects of the old stage of organisation yet continue to use some of their sufficient aspects, often in a modified form. Thus, an earlier stage is conceivable without a later one but not vice versa. In this respect, the stages are in hierarchical order, but not in the sense of the hierarchy of an evaluation that includes degradation of earlier stages. This would be viewing the whole system only from the hierarchical stage.

Difference 3: There Is a Final Stage of the Evolution of Consciousness That Can Already Be Outlined

The model introduced here includes one final stage, and it is asserted that no further evolution is required. Graves, on the other hand, was convinced that the process of evolution cannot in principle lead to the highest stage but that every stage will lead to yet another. In this respect, he was not determined by evolutionary optimism, as later stages could certainly produce new negative sides and the evils of the world could simply continue to run free in other dimensions without the world getting closer to a long-term solution.

My approach takes for its premise that man is capable of attaining a state of consciousness that does not require another rise, as in a fear-less state we are capable of mastering all new challenges with compo-sure and the greatest possible measure of intelligence and creativity. If a sufficiently great number of people should become acquainted with this state and act from that place, a cultural stage is possible that will bring about a political and economic order that can guarantee for lasting peace and levelled affluence.

Difference 4: The Fifth Stage in Particular Is Reformulated in Many Ways

As for this stage (green), Graves and his interpreters had thought of the exponents of alternative ways of living from the second half of the 19th century onwards (e.g. Henry David Thoreau). Key terms create a novel sense of community, human solidarity, ecological sensitivity and the creation of social networks. According to my model, these aspects already belong to the systemic stage. The term personalism is inter-preted historico-culturally to a greater extent and is identified in many aspects of modern art but also in the genesis and rise of modern psychology. It is a bridge from materialism to systemic consciousness, which in my opinion seems quite colourless and not very nuanced in Graves' model while in mine it is granted a concise status.

Further Reading

General remarks on these references:

This survey is incomplete for two reasons. This book was fuelled by many ideas and concepts which the author owes to others, often without being able to trace the origins in particular. As the topic is very widely stretched, it can be deepened and broadened in every aspect so that there could be lots of references to each paragraph and chapter. The following list should rather serve readers who want to gain more insight in some of the aspects touched in this book.

Evolution of consciousness in general:

Gregory Bateson (2000): Steps to an Ecology of Mind. University of Chicago Press
Beck, Don Edwards (2005): Cowan, Christopher C.: Spiral Dynamics: Mastering Values, Leadership and Change. Blackwell Publishers
Jürgen Habermas (1979): Communication and the Evolution of Society. Beacon Press
Georg Wilhelm Friedrich Hegel (1976): Phenomenology of Spirit. Oxford University Press
Lawrence Kohlberg (1981): The Philosophy of Moral Development: Moral Stages and the Idea of Justice. Harper & Row
Steve McIntosh (2007): Integral Consciousness and the Future of Evolution: How the Integral Worldview Is Transforming Politics, Culture, and Spirituality. Continuum-3pl
Ken Wilber (2007): Integral Spirituality: A Startling New Role for Religion in the Modern and Postmodern World. Shambhala

The Organic foundations:

Antonio Damasio (1999): The Feeling of What Happens. Harvest
Stanislav Grof (1993): The Holotropic Mind: The Three Levels of Human Consciousness and How They Shape Our Lives. HarperOne
Steven Pinker (1999): How the Mind Works. Penguin
Stephen W. Porges (2011): The Polyvagal Theory: Neurophysiological Foundations of Emotions, Attachment, Communication, and Self-regulation. W. W. Norton & Company

Ernest Lawrence Rossi (1993): The Psychobiology of Mind-Body Healing: New Concepts of Therapeutic Hypnosis. W. W. Norton & Company
Jeffrey Satinover (2001): The Quantum Brain. The Search for Freedom and the Next Generation of Man. John Wiley & Sons
Daniel N. Stern (2000): The Interpersonal World Of The Infant A View From Psychoanalysis And Developmental Psychology. Basic Books

Stage 1:

Brian Bates (2005): The Way of Wyrd. Hay House
Mircea Eliade (2004): Shamanism: Archaic Techniques of Ecstasy. Princeton University Press
Serge Kahili King (1990): Urban Shaman. Touchstone
Jean Jacques Rousseau (1968): The Social Contract. Penguin Classics

Stage 2:

Robert Bly (1992): Iron John: A Book About Men. Vintage Books
Homer (1998): The Iliad. Penguin Classics
Sam Keen (1992): Fire in the Belly. On Being a Man. Bantam
Gabriel Garcia Marquez (2006): One Hundred Years of Solitude. Harper Perennial Modern Classics
William Hansen (2005): Classical Mythology: A Guide to the Mythical World of the Greeks and Romans. Oxford University Press

Stage 3:

Hannah Arendt (1973): The Origins of Totalitarianism. Harvest Books
Norbert Elias (2000): The Civilizing Process: Sociogenetic and Psychogenetic Investigations. Blackwell Publishing
Michel Foucault (1995): Discipline & Punish: The Birth of the Prison. Vintage Books
Franz Kafka (1987): The Trial. Schocken
Stanislav Lem (1985): The Futurological Congress. Mariner
Herta Müller (2009): Atemschaukel . Hanser
George Orwell (2000): Homage to Catalonia. Penguin
Platon (2000): The Republic. Dover Publications

Stage 4:

Walter Benjamin (2008): The Work of Art in the Age of Its Technological Reproducibility. Belknap Press
René Descartes (1956): Discourse on Method. Pearson
Wolfgang Fritz Haug (1987): Commodity Aesthetics, Ideology and Culture. Intl General
Daniel Kehlmann (2007): Measuring the World. Vintage
Karl Marx (1988): The Economic and Philosophic Manuscripts of 1844. Prometheus
Pier Paolo Pasolini (1992): Freibeuterschriften. Wagenbach
Adam Smith (2003): The Wealth of Nations. Bantam Classics
Alfred Sohn-Rethel (1978): Intellectual and Manual Labour: Critique of Epistemology. Macmillan
Max Weber (2001): The Protestant Ethic and the Spirit of Capitalism. Routledge

Stage 5:

Aurelius Augustinus (2009): Confessions. Oxford University Press
Sigmund Freud (1989): Introductory Lectures on Psychoanalysis. Liveright
Robert Fritz (1989): Path of Least Resistance. Ballantine Books
Stanislav Grof (1985): Beyond the Brain: Birth, Death, and Transendence in Psychotherapy. State University of New York Press
Sören Kierkegaard (1986): Fear and Trembling. Penguin Classics
Heinz Kohut (2014): The Restauration of the Self. University Of Chicago Press
Abraham H. Maslow (1970): Motivation and Personality. Harper & Row
Friedrich Nietzsche (1978): A Nietzsche Reader. Penguin Classics
Carl R. Rogers (1995): On Becoming a Person: A Therapist's View of Psychotherapy. Mariner Books
Jean Paul Sartre (2007): Existentialism Is a Humanism. Yale University Press

Stage 6:

Bert Hellinger (1998): Love's Hidden Symmetry: What Makes Love Work in Relationships. Zeig, Tucker & Theisen

Paul Feyerabend (1975): Against Method : Outline of an Anarchistic Theory of Knowledge. Radner & S. Winokur
Michel Foucault (1994): The Order of Things: An Archaeology of the Human Sciences. Vintage
Alexandre Jardin (1999): L'Ile de gauchers. Editions Flammarion
Humberto R. Maturana, Francisco J. Varela (1992): Tree of Knowledge. Shambala
Niklas Luhmann (2010): Introduction to Systems Theory. Polity
Marshall B. Rosenberg (2003): Nonviolent Communication: A Language of Life. Puddledancer Press
Peter Sloterdijk (1988): Critique of Cynical Reason. University Of Minnesota Press
Insa Sparrer (2007): Miracle, Solution and System. Solutions Books
Paul Watzlawick, Janet H. Beavin, Don D. Jackson (2000): Pragmatics of Human Communication: A Study of Interactional Patterns, Pathologies, and Paradoxes. W. W. Norton & Company
Paul Watzlawick (1977): How Real Is Real? Vintage
Ludwig Wittgenstein (1998): Tractatus logico-philosophicus. Dover Publications
(2009): Philosophical Investigations. Wiley-Blackwe

Stage 7:

Ramesh Balsekar (1999): Who Cares?! Advaita Press
David Brazier (1995): Zen Therapy. Constable
Mihaly Csikszentmihalyi (2008): Flow: The Psychology of Optimal Experience. Harper Perennial Modern Classics
Karlfried Graf Dürckheim (2004): Hara. The Vital Center of Man. Inner Traditions
Grant McFetridge (2004): Peak States of Consciousness: Volume I, Breakthrough Techniques for Exceptional Quality of Life. Institute for the Studies of Peakstates
(2008): Peak States of Consciousness: Theory and Applications, Volume 2: Acquiring Extraordinary Spiritual and Shamanic States. Institute for the Studies of Peakstates Press
S.N. Goenka (1987): The Discourse Summaries. Vipassana Research Institute

Maitreya Ishwara (2002): Unity. The Dawn of Conscious Civilization. Divine Publications

Jack Kornfield (1993): A Path with Heart. A Guide Through the Perils and Promises of Spiritual Life. Bantam

Joy Manné (1997): Soul Therapy. North Atlantic Books

Melvin E. Miller and Susanne R. Cook-Greuter (2000): Creativity, Spirituality and Transcendence. Ablex Publishing Corporation

Sogyal Rinpoche (1994): The Tibetan Book of Living and Dying. Random House

Eckhart Tolle (1999): The Power of Now. A Guide to Spiritual Enlightenment. Hodder & Stoughton

About the Author

Wilfried Ehrmann, PhD, studied philosophy, psychology and history, training in different approaches of therapy, licensed psychotherapist in Vienna, Austria, seminar leader and lecturer in different countries, trainer in integrative breathwork in Austria and other countries, author (book and articles) and blogger.

http://www.wilfried-ehrmann.com

Zeitfracht Medien GmbH
Ferdinand-Jühlke-Straße 7
99095 Erfurt, Deutschland
produktsicherheit@kolibri360.de